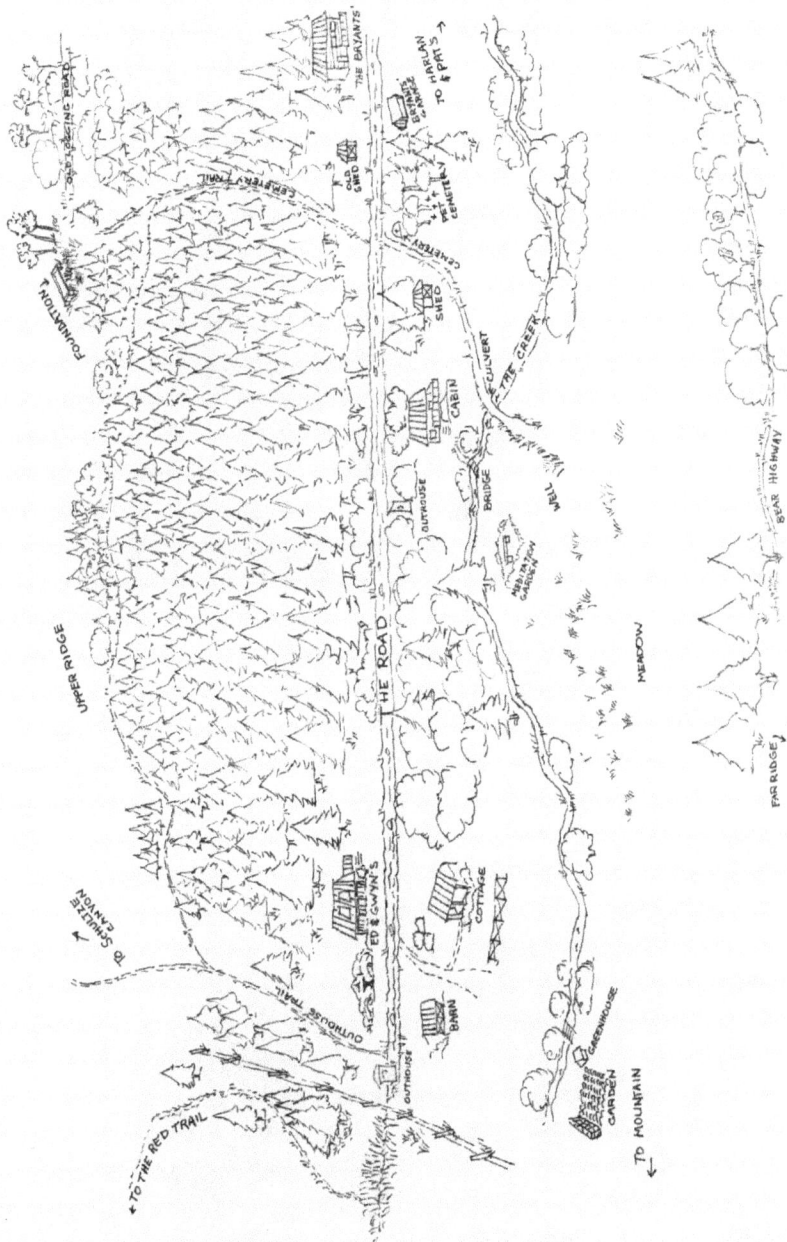

BURN SCARS

A Memoir of the Land and Its Loss

Patricia Prijatel

First Printing: 2020

Clementine Press: Des Moines, Iowa; Walsenburg, Colorado
ISBN 978-0-578-65820-9

For questions, requests, special discounts and bulk orders, please contact the author at "contacts" at patriciaprijatel.com

For wildfire fighters everywhere,
especially those who fought the East Peak Fire.
For Harlan, who told them we were there.
And for Ross, who was a very good dog.

"We are called to assist the Earth to heal her wounds
And in the process heal our own."

Wangari Maathai
2004 Nobel Peace Prize Lecture

Contents

Prologue: *The Sacred Mountain*   *1*

Part One: *The Land and the Fire*

1. *A Dry and Brittle Land*   *7*

2. *Forest Bathing*   *13*

3. *The Valley of Friends*   *17*

4. *Escape*   *25*

5. *There Can't Be Anything Left*   *33*

6. *In a Forest Fire, Pecan Pie Is Often Sadly Overlooked*   *37*

7. *We Feel Like Cowards. We Feel Sane*   *47*

8. *Walking Sideways*   *51*

9. *A Voluptuous Land*   *59*

10. *I Revere This Place*   *69*

11. *Sleeping with an Ear to the Creek*   *73*

12. *Communal Grief*   *83*

Part Two: *A Stressed Earth and its Creatures*

13. *I Didn't Expect Fear*   *91*

14. *The Bear: A Premonition*   *99*

15. *Walking Through a Poem*   *101*

16. *Boulders Shifting*   *111*

17. *The Bear*   *117*

18. *Warning: Do Not Crack*   *133*

19. *Our Bodies Break*   *141*

Part Three: ***Climate Grief***

20. *Yellow Fingernails* **151**

21. *Resurrection* **161**

22. *Burn Scars* **165**

23. *Shade We'll Never Sit In* **171**

24. *Pockets of Gorgeous Hope* **179**

Notes **193**

Acknowledgements **201**

The Sacred Mountain

The locals call them the breasts of the earth, or *Wahatoya*, using the Comanche word. Geologists call them the Spanish Peaks. The great twin mountains, the East Spanish Peak and the West Spanish Peak, rise up from the high desert of Southern Colorado, alone and distinct, their own separate mountain range. Breasts emerging from the earth.

The East Peak rises to 12,683 feet; the West Peak to 13,625 feet. Two natural pyramids reflecting the azure of the Colorado sky.

The geological highlights of the Spanish Peaks are the immense and stunning walls of rock, or dikes, that radiate from the peaks for miles at widths from a foot to 100 feet. The largest, the Big Wall, stretches 14 miles from the West Peak toward the town of La Veta, looking like a natural version of the Great Wall of China. Dikes are rock walls that formed 25 million or so years ago when volcanic activity broke cracks in the earth—earthquakes—through which lava flowed, filling the gaps with molten rock, which then dried, creating underground walls. The bigger the quake, the bigger the dike. As the ground eroded, the walls began to emerge, and through millions of years, the resulting structures, the dikes, grew into formations that are the focal point of the land around the peaks. Some dikes remain underground, some barely break through the earth, and some create awe-inspiring ramparts that dominate the landscape like mythical vestiges of an ancient land. Scientists come from around the world to study these geological marvels. Geologists have counted at least 400 separate dikes around the two peaks.

The Comanches and Utes who once lived here believed the mountains were sacred and those who lived in their shadow were blessed. It feels holy here.

After the East Peak fire of 2013 burned 13,500 acres of the mountain's mostly forested land, we're praying for a resurrection. Our prayers are not being answered the way we'd hoped.

PART ONE

The Land and the Fire

1. A Dry and Brittle Land

I'm standing at 11,000 feet on the East Spanish Peak, balancing my legs on the two flattest rocks I can find. At this altitude the landscape abruptly switches from scraggly evergreens to sun-bleached boulders. I take a long drink of water, exhale slowly to catch my breath, then inhale and survey my perch.

Below, the view extends from mountain forests—a pointillist sketch of silvery blue, neon green, emerald, and jade—to the wispy blue plateaus of eastern Colorado. The scent of the forest has faded with the pines we left behind, but I detect a faintly recognizable fragrance. I inhale again, short breaths of the thin air. Then I realize what it is: the smell of fresh, unadulterated air warmed by the sun.

The granite under my feet soaks up the September rays and creates the aroma of the Earth itself. I stretch my neck and raise my head and feel the warmth on my face, feel the Sun and the Earth anchor me here, in this spot, on this mountain.

We're all alone up here, my husband, Joe, and I. The quiet is enormous.

In the meadow below, I spot our cabin, our neighbor's log home, and my brother and sister-in-law's lodge, barn, and guesthouse. Their green tin roofs look like Monopoly pieces scattered in the grass 3,000 feet beneath us.

The ridges are verdant waterfalls, with evergreens fanning out and cascading toward the meadow. But the warning signs are there. The meadow is yellowing from lack of rain and the forest is pockmarked with dead trees, the handiwork of pine beetles and the drought we've been fighting off and on for the nearly two decades we've had land here. Every summer, we cut more damaged trees, but the beetles are always a step ahead of us.

This eagle's view of our dangerously vulnerable mountain sanctuary worries me. One hot, dry summer after another has left a brittle forest susceptible to nature's worst instincts: fire and wind. The threat of fire is so real we have planned our evacuation routes. If the burn starts above us, we can take the road that follows the meadow down the mountain. If it starts below us, that's a bit more ominous, and we'd have to use four-wheel-drive to get us to one of the logging roads that climb over the ridges. If the wind is low, the fire will burn slower and we'll have more time to get out.

Yet, while we consider risks and threats and escape, these are theoretical, back-of-the-mind *what if*s. We blithely live our lives as though this will always be here, like this, only better if only we could get some rain.

Facts tell us otherwise.

The American West is warming at a rate 70 percent higher than the rest of the world, with an average increase in temperature of 1.7 degrees just in the four years from 2003 to 2007. Most of the area's warming has occurred since the 1970s, part of a worldwide pattern in which each month since 1984 has been warmer than normal.

This has led to less snowfall, earlier snow melt, more winter rain, and reduced summer precipitation. Warmer spring and summer temperatures increase wildfire risk and the proliferation of the pine beetles that weaken entire forests.

We feel and see this change as it is happening—we're right in the middle of it.

But, to us, being here is a reward that is more than worth the risk. We acknowledge the threat, but don't entirely believe it.

Joe and I started our hike up here at 6 a.m., wanting to make sure we'd climb when it is coolest and before any afternoon storms. Our goal is to make it to the bowl, the gigantic spoon-shaped dent right above tree line, carved by eons of erosion.

It's 9:30 a.m. September 19, 2012. Ten months, two days, and 15 hours before fire will drive us off out of this paradise, before this green turns black. This is the last year of this beauty, the last year of the mountain feeling safe.

We climb steadily along Bear Creek, the only sound the rushing stream and the *clip, clip, clip* of my hiking stick. Our backpacks are full of water, energy bars, and fruit. We get to the White Trail that will take us up the mountain, and it looks so ordinary, a simple mountain path, up a little slope tucked inside a canopy of evergreens. Soon, though, it gets rocky and steep. Every 15 feet or so, I have to stop and breathe because of the ascent and the thin air.

Finally, we rest for a snack. Joe sits on a fallen aspen and I settle on a reasonably smooth rock. I dig through my backpack for energy bars and give us each one. The packages rattle like plastic leaves rustling in the wind, unnatural and intrusive. The first bar is so good—crunchy nut, dried fruit, and chocolate— we have a second. The sound of our chewing reverberates against the backdrop of silent woods.

We don't talk much as we hike because I have moderate emphysema and simply breathing takes what energy I have. Joe, eight years my senior, could chat my leg off while scrabbling effortlessly up the hill. He's a nice man, though, so he keeps quiet and walks slowly to suit pokey me. We catch up with conversation when we stop.

"It's just around the next bend," he says, an old joke. Our destination is almost always eight or a thousand bends away, but he promises—over and over—that we're just about there.

We finish our bars and share a banana. We're in the midst of a thick, old forest, part of the Earth's lungs, absorbing carbon dioxide and fighting climate change. It's a blend of towering firs, pines, spruce, and aspens, diverse and rich.

"How high are we?" I ask.

Joe checks his GPS watch. "Almost 9500 feet."

"Another thousand feet or so," I say.

"Just around the bend," he repeats.

I snort fetchingly.

A breeze whispers by and the aspen leaves quiver.

"Ready to go again?" he asks.

"Ready," I say, taking several deep breaths to prepare for the next stretch.

We jam our garbage into the backpack, I grab my stick, and we get back on the trail. *Clip, clip, clip.*

We reach the bowl at mid-morning, a three-hour hike that would have taken Joe alone probably two.

"We made it," I say, hugging him.

"Yes. And we don't ever have to do it again," he says with a chuckle. He tries to kiss me, but the bills of our hats collide so we have to turn our heads diagonally to reach one another's lips. It's quick, gentle, sweet, graceless.

"Do you want to go the rest of the way to the peak? We could probably see New Mexico from the top." That would mean another 2,000 feet or so of hiking, all on rocks, some the size of Army tanks.

"I've seen New Mexico," he says.

"Fair enough." Also, *thank God.*

Hand in hand, we straddle the rocky terrain, balancing carefully as we survey the bowl, going up a bit, then over, but the rocks are unforgiving, so we head back to a grove of evergreens on the edge. There, we can see the tin roof of the miner's shack, a destination point for many who climb this peak. It's a wooden structure about 10 feet square, built probably a hundred years ago. Our neighbor Fiore's dad and uncles used donkeys to carry materials up the mountain, built the cabin, then cut nearby trees so they could see down to the homes where their wives and children lived. The mine they dug is supposedly to the east. It yielded only rocks and sand. No gold.

A rusted roof covers the cabin's log walls. The door is open; inside, old newspapers, cans, boxes and other debris fill the hard dirt floor. In the middle stands a wood stove, with a cast iron frying pan on top. It's musty, with a whiff of dead animal. And silent—no birds, no wind, no creatures. Just us.

"Imagine trying to live up here," I say, picking up the frying pan, then replacing it on the stove. *Clank.*

"No," Joe says. "Our cabin is rustic enough."

We go back outside and walk in what we assume is the direction of the mine. The trees are tall and thin and the ground a soft gravel, but we're going downhill, which means we'll have to come back up again. Not me. I'm done with climbing for this day.

"I really don't need to see the mine," I say. "I'll wait for you here."

"No," he says emphatically. "I don't need to see it either."

We walk out of the grove and find a couple of rocks where we can sit for a while, savor the view, and have a drink and a celebratory granola bar. Then we slowly climb back down the mountain, my walking stick again accompanying us with its melodic clicks.

We're back at the cabin in time for a late lunch. We rest on the deck with iced tea and peanut butter and jelly sandwiches because that's all we have the energy to make. I dig out the binoculars and peer up the mountain. I try to see the miner's shack or the trail we were on, but it is all hidden in the trees. In less than a year, fire will savagely open up the view. The trees will be gone but we'll still not see the shack, as it too will burn.

2. Forest Bathing

We've not had what we consider an official rain—one that wets the entire deck—for weeks. We often get showers with 16 or so drops that remind us how wonderful rain smells and then it all blows over. The grass withers to a crisp, the trees droop, and the creek dries up.

Joe and I go for an early morning hike along the foothills near the cabin. These wanderings are why we're here: to experience this land, to smell it and hear it and see it from as many angles as we can. We climb up from our meadow, along the forested ridge at 8,000 feet, into Schultz Canyon, then back onto our land and up a fairly arduous hill to home. We never lose sight of the mountain, the quiet guardian of our land. It's one of our favorite walks, just under three miles.

We keep an eye on the trees swaying in the wind, wondering about the prospect of more serious gusts, which have become common in recent years. It can get so windy on the mountain that pieces of our houses—usually parts of the roofs of our outbuildings—fly onto the neighbors' land. Once our outhouse came completely off its perch near the road and blew about 200 feet down the meadow, landing on its side, intact, like a Barbie outhouse in the grass. As if Barbie would ever have an outhouse. Afterward, as I sat inside working at my desk, I watched Joe walk by carrying the rustic old shell on his shoulders from the inside, like an outhouse with legs, and calmly put it back into place.

The temperature climbs as the sun rolls higher into the sky, but the wind is a cooling relief.

The Japanese have a concept called *shinrin-yoku*, roughly translated as *forest bathing*. It originated in 1982 when the country's forest agency began to encourage wellbeing to combat the threat of suicide in Japan, which at that time was the highest in the world. The idea is to walk deliberately and slowly in the woods, observing, breathing, and appreciating. The result is a drop in blood pressure and in cortisol, a stress hormone.

Our walks in this land are pure *shinrin-yoku*. We bathe in the light, the air, the calm of nature.

The views are everything on this hike: vast stretches of mountain grass, thick forests, rock outcroppings. And, always, the mountain. We sometimes run into elk and bears along the way. They always dash off, elegant and silent, when they see us.

The silence of the land is one of the things I treasure most here. It's so quiet we can hear the grass rustle in the wind on the other side of the meadow. No cars, no cellphone conversations, no bass sounds from some kid's stereo, no blasted leaf blowers. Conservationists are fighting to preserve America's wild spaces to quiet the country's jittery nerves. The quality of what they call our "soundscape" is a measure of our stress. Quiet places in nature are calming. Cities are perpetually tense. Our land, I believe, is one of the quietest places on earth.

As we walk, we pass my sister-in-law Gwyn's favorite tree—a giant Douglas fir in a perfect pyramid shape, a horticulturist's dream that grows alone and naturally in the canyon. We all have favorite trees here. Mine is a majestic Colorado blue spruce across the meadow from the cabin: tall, thin, regal, and home to an enormous owl. My brother Ed's is a ponderosa pine along the Red Trail. He's been known to hug his tree, but only to measure its girth. He's 77 inches tall and the tree is at least a third wider than his reach. Joe actually loves any aspen but is especially fond of the babies that sprout along the hillside opposite the cabin.

It's June 19, 2013. We have no inkling that a fire is quietly smoldering in the rocks high above us. The sky is a crystal clear, cloudless Colorado blue. We feel safe, sheltered, and comforted. Soon most of this green will be black, the sky filled with menacing smoke. But our favorite trees will survive: Gwyn's Douglas fir, Ed's ponderosa pine, my Colorado blue spruce. And Joe's aspens will be the fierce little fighters of the fire. Aspen groves, especially young ones, can actually be fire buffers, stopping a fire in its tracks. Plus, because entire groves share one underground root, aspens usually grow new shoots quickly after a fire, so the neon green aspen trees are the first new growth in a burned forest.

We've named our trails: The Cemetery Trail starts on the road past our little aspen grove that holds Mom and Dad's and Gwyn's mother's ashes. It's also where five of Ed and Gwyn's dogs are buried. Our little dog, Simon, is there too.

Dominic's Road, up the far ridge, is named for the neighbor who helped build it.

The Outhouse Trail starts at Ed and Gwyn's old outhouse that has the best view of any toilet in the world.

The Benches are by Doc's house, a neighbor we've never met with a pentagonal house overlooking the valley, with wooden benches lining the edge of a rock cliff.

Over the Dike goes up the meadow toward the mountain, over a hill it took us 10 years to realize was actually a dike because most of it remains covered in earth and trees; we walk back to the cabin along the creek.

We've done them all this year, except the Red Trail and I had been thinking of suggesting that for tomorrow. I don't yet know, of course, that we will not be here tomorrow, that the Red Trail will be in flames. That hike is 4.5 miles, along the side of the mountain, and is spectacular, with remarkable views of our valley, storybook trails along the creek, and quite a few challenging hills.

We usually come to the mountain in late May or June to catch the wildflowers of early summer. Wild iris and geraniums fill the meadow with a lush throw of lavender and pink amidst a hundred different shades of green. Wild roses and columbines, Colorado's state flower, poke up in happy bands along the creek. Even in drought years, spring and early summer can be green because of recent snowmelt.

This is a semi-arid climate, and droughts are common, usually becoming more severe in the summer and breaking a bit in the fall and winter. In June 2013, the majority of Colorado, including our own Huerfano County, is in extreme drought and has been for nearly three years. At the roots of our meadow grass, the earth is chalky and dry. Little puffs of dust erupt if we hit the ground too forcefully with our boots, which soon are covered with dust.

The rest of the day after our walk is full of normal chores and relaxation. We have lunch on the deck, watching the mountain. Joe takes a nap in his hammock; he calls it reading. I rest inside, with the windows open to the fresh air. Anne Lamott says she thinks God smells like a young child's slightly dirty neck. I say God smells like mountain air. And as we putter outdoors pulling weeds and trimming branches, I take photos of the iris, roses, bluebells, and geraniums.

Joe and I have been on the mountain since June 3. Thirteen days. Long enough to have wandered all over our 200 acres and into the neighbors', toward the mountain, over the ridges, exercising our bodies and calming our souls, giving us time to chat and examine the land.

It's the last we time we will ever see it like this.

3. The Valley of Friends

I t's usually just the four of us this far up in the valley—me, Joe, Ed, and Gwyn—plus the bears, elk, coyotes, deer, eagles, and occasional lost strangers. Our two little settlements are at the end of a dirt and boulder road at the foot of the East Spanish Peak.

We're summer people, Joe and I in our handmade cabin, Ed and Gwyn up the road in their mini-ranch. Our land in this mountain valley is our dream, a legacy from our parents who didn't want to leave their children money when they died but wanted to see what we would do with it while they were still living. They didn't have much—Dad was a steelworker at the Colorado Fuel and Iron steel plant and Mom sometimes worked in snooty dress stores, but more often stayed home and raised her five kids, of which I am the youngest.

When Mom and Dad gave the five of us their hard-earned money as their legacy, it offered me the chance to own mountain land, and I never considered another option. The mountains have always been my comfort and my solace. I spent my first 21 years in the working-class city of Pueblo, 50 miles north of the Spanish Peaks, but the Colorado Rockies nurtured me. My long legs grew strong and solid by hiking animal trails along creeks and up to waterfalls. My curiosity blossomed through studying mountain ranges and wondering how they got there. My spirit thrived on the smell of pines after a rain and the sounds of wind breathing through the cottonwoods.

When I was signing papers to buy this place, even then I knew this land would own me, and not the other way around. I often talk about "our mountain," but by that I mean I'm part of it and it's a part of me. We're in this together. I agree with Native Americans who say that we are left this land in trust, as caretakers, and our responsibility is to bequeath it to our grandchildren in as healthy shape as we got it—or more so.

In 1992 Ed, our sister Phyllis, and I bought our parcel, part of what had been a working ranch, used primarily for cattle grazing. Phyllis reluctantly pulled out after a few years because she had too much on her plate already and sold her land to Ed, but she and her kids helped us build all our homes up here. Our brother John used part of his gift to buy land closer to Pueblo and on a far better road; our sister Kay put hers toward retirement.

Mom died a year after we bought our land and saw it only once, for a family picnic on a warm October afternoon. Dad came up several times, watching us build, going for short walks; he was in his 80s then, and not the vibrant mountain hiker he had been as a younger man. But his whip-smart brain was still sparking and he was captivated by what we were doing. He had built his own house in Pueblo in 1937, so he knew home construction, and he helped advise our contractor—Ed. He lived long enough to see at least Ed and Gwyn's small barn, the first structure we built up here.

This is friendly country, and the year-round residents—the nearby ranchers—are dear to us. The friendships we have made with Harlan and Pat down the road two miles, Pearl and Fiore at the bottom of the switchback, and Dave and his family one canyon over, are warm, satisfying. We try to blend in with their way of doing things, take their lead, because they know this land better than we do.

One of Pearl and Fiori's sons lives within sight of their house, two grandsons and their families live within a few miles, and a cousin's house is down the road. That's the pattern in this area of southern Colorado—farmers and ranchers moved in two or three generations ago, bought a little land, then some more and then some more, had kids, then grandkids, many of whom stayed on the land, expanding their own ranches and families. These are truly working farmers and ranchers, not absentee owners.

•   •   •

Our tranquil mountain valley is about as remote as you can get in today's America. It's a mile from San Isabel National Forest and about a 45-minute drive south of Walsenburg. Taos is an easy day trip. Property here is measured in hundreds, often thousands, of acres. With only 35 acres, Joe and I are a little dot on the home-ownership map. Ed and Gwyn have 165 acres.

Our property is shaped like a fat, upside down "L," with the two sides a mile long and nearly a half-mile thick. We built our houses along the meadow between two ridges that crawl up to the East Spanish Peak.

For years I have wanted to get a sign for the entrance to our land: *Dolina Prijateljev,* or *The Valley of Friends* in Slovene. My last name, Prijatel, means *friend* in Slovene, and three of our grandparents emigrated from that beautiful Alpine country; the fourth came from neighboring Croatia. I like to think they would be pleased where their grandchildren settled, a little valley that looks a lot like Slovenia.

Ed always wanted a ranch—he said *wrench* when we were kids—and he and Gwyn have built a beautiful little one up here. The house is a work of art, a modern chalet built into the hillside, with cedar shingles and an asymmetrical metal roof, with one long line covering a three-car garage. Inside are hardwood floors, skylights, stained-glass windows, French doors, sloped ceilings, and handcrafted tiles around the wood-burning stove and in the kitchen.

Across the road and down a few steps are the barn on the right and a guest cottage on the left. The barn has two stalls, enough for Czarina, Gwyn's stately black Tennessee Walking Horse, and an equine visitor. Gwyn is an artist and her artwork is everywhere on the mountain, most charmingly in a portrait of a horse looking through a window, which she painted on the windowless barn.

The guest cottage has window boxes that Gwyn keeps overflowing with thick, multicolored bouquets of petunias, pansies, and geraniums. The four of us often sit and chat for hours on the long front porch, watching the mountain do nothing in its own beautiful way. It may be the most relaxing place on Earth. Our cabin deck is a close second.

The creek is at the bottom of the hill—a thin gurgle that snakes through the grass and borders the meadow. Next to it, Gwyn has built a high-altitude vegetable garden, with lettuce, carrots, green beans, peppers, kale, cabbage, broccoli, cauliflower, and anything else you might need for vegetative sustenance. It's protected from the wind, sun, and animals by a four-foot wall on the mountain side and a high fence elsewhere.

Ed and Gwyn did it all, even the stained glass, with the help of their sons Matt and Pat, and a host of nieces, nephews, and friends. To get approved by the building inspector, Ed had to have his garage doors installed by an outside contractor. He insists he could have done that too. And he is probably right. In many things, he can do it all.

In the winter, Ed and Gwyn live in Monument, north of Colorado Springs, with a view of the Air Force Academy. They spend April to November here. They share their lives with Ross, a giant rescue dog, and Bella, a petite Labrador retriever.

They work hard up here, and they have the backs to prove it; both need regular steroid shots and pain pills.

It takes about five minutes to walk from Ed and Gwyn's ranch to our cabin, about a quarter of a mile away, and downhill about 100 feet. The road is rimmed with towering pines and firs, aspens, locust bushes, and scrub oak. It reminds me of an illustration my parents had hanging on the wall in the basement, of Joyce Kilmer's *Trees,* the poem typeset into a tunnel of trees, probably cut out of a magazine.

A 1940s Case tractor that doesn't run and that came with the property marks the beginning of what might be considered our yard. When we built the cabin, we chose this spot because of the creek, plus the view of the mountain on the right, the meadow and ridge in front, the high desert in the distance on the left.

My mantra when we were building was, "It's just a mountain cabin." I wanted to spend my time here hiking and watching nature, not building. Plus, I wanted to leave as small a footprint as possible. So, pretty much, it's just a mountain cabin, but a beautiful welcoming home and I truly love it. The housing appraiser called it a "friendly little place" and Phyllis says it reminds her of a dollhouse. I had originally tried calling it a cottage, but that never took. It insisted on being a cabin.

Ed and his son Matt built the main part: the exterior, a simple 480-square-foot rectangle—20X24-feet—with the green metal roof that has become the Prijatel mountain signature. It's 20 inches off the ground, built on pilings, or elevated posts, of cement blocks reinforced with concrete and rebar.

Our son, Josh, and I built the front deck and we're both pleased it still stands; it's sort of trapezoidal and has some huge gaps between the boards, but it works. Joe and Josh built a side deck, and my nephew Dan built a corner deck connecting the two. So we have a wrap-around deck that only took about 15 years and two generations from three families to complete.

Our daughter, Ellen, did just about everything—helping Ed with electrical and plumbing, hammering up the trim, painting the walls and floor, installing the sink. She spent several months at the cabin alone after graduating from college, mixing cement, working on finishing touches, hiking, relaxing, and recharging.

We all had a hand in the interior walls. I wanted a textured finish, so Gwyn went down to the creek and got sand, which we mixed with the paint. Josh and Ellen put the drywall on the ceiling. We painted the walls a salmon color that reflects the sun, with white trim and sage doors.

I often sit in bed, reading, looking at the walls and ceiling and smiling at their lovable imperfections—plaster lines than were never smoothed over completely, trim that doesn't quite line up. I love it all. Both of our children are so much with me at that cabin because so much of them is in it, even though Ellen now lives in Vermont and Josh in Istanbul.

Our kitchen cabinets are white vintage cupboards with the original round copper hardware. Gwyn spotted them in the antique store and told me, "There's your kitchen." And, yes, there it was, and here it now is. The coffee table is a wooden icebox my dad made sometime in the 1950s, which we used for camping all over the Colorado Rockies. The heavy wood toolbox he lugged all over Pueblo when he built his house is a side table and sits under a somewhat garish mirror I got from their house after they died. The bed is a walnut four-poster that Joe and I bought at Goodwill when we were first married in 1970.

Our golden-brown sofa opens to a queen bed and takes up most of one wall. Next to it is a cabin-sized Queen Anne recliner, which is where I both read and write. A round oak table takes up the middle of the room, with an extra leaf hidden behind the couch for the many times we have family and friends over for dinner. My mom's old rocking chair is snuggled into one corner and is Joe's favorite place to read.

If I could have a do-over on the cabin, I would have more windows, but those we have light up the place like a welcoming lantern.

We're all off the grid, with solar power, propane gas, composting toilets, and well water. Joe and I have only two solar panels and Ed and Gwyn have eight, so they have more creature comforts than we do, such as TV and microwave. But ours is just a mountain cabin. Our only utility is the phone line and that is erratic. Cell coverage is minimal because we're in a mountain valley. Being here forces us to unplug. Ah, sanity.

We have a 35-gallon water tank that we fill up once a day, and a 5-gallon hot water tank, so no long showers for us. Our bathroom has a tub, but we don't have enough hot water to fill it to soaking temperature. Not all visitors are fans of the compost toilet, so we have a little outhouse with a plastic camping toilet, a bottle of water to help with flushing, and wet wipes for hand washing. When we expect guests, I make sure there is a bouquet of flowers at the front, and I clean out the wasps that like to nest in the toilet lid. The outhouse has only three sides—the front is open— and it's in a grove of locust and pine trees for privacy. It has a killer view.

Our deck faces the meadow and the mountain, with the back of the cabin to the road. The only people who ever use the road are family, friends, or people who are lost, usually looking for the scout camp. We have to tell campers they can't get there from here, that no matter what Google says, our road is a dead end.

We live at the cabin from June through September and then go back to our full-time home in Iowa for the winter.

I never intended to stay in Iowa when I moved there to work for *Better Homes and Gardens* books in 1968 after I graduated from college. But I fell in love with Joe and we settled into kids and houses and jobs. I eventually was hired to head the magazine journalism program at Drake University, a gem of a job, through which I met students and faculty and community members who became good friends and part of a great life.

Being at the cabin four months of the year gives me my mountain fix. Iowa gives me the rest.

While I taught, I could spend only a part of the summer on the mountain. I longed for more time here, so in 2008, I retired early.

When I am not here, I carry this land with me.

4. Escape

I am sitting in what we mockingly call my office—a small kneehole desk set diagonally in a corner banked by windows on either side. It's early evening and soft rays of sun break through the trees behind the cabin, gently gilding the meadow and the mountain. It's a serene, blessed time of day.

At least a dozen raptors glide in the currents above the ridge, where the trees are full of their enormous nests. The wind is picking up and coating our furniture with a grimy film of dust from the thirsty ground.

I am at the desk drawing, starting a picture book for our grandson Eli's third birthday, about the pirate on the mountain. I can see the pirate from the window as I study the mountain, a formation of trees and rocks that create a Johnny Depp sort of swashbuckler, with features defined by 50-foot ponderosa pines poking out of granite skin. He has a pert nose, neat beard, and a large, graceful hat; one eye squints and the other one is covered with a patch.

Joe is making dinner, cutting fresh broccoli, cauliflower, and mushrooms in the kitchen at the other end of the cabin, 15 feet or so from me. He has poured himself some wine. I am sipping cheap bourbon—a bad decision at the liquor store the day before.

The phone on the desk, about a foot from me, rings. I answer.

"Bad news," Ed says. I sit up straighter. Alert. Wary.

"Fire at the scout camp," he continues. My hand grasps the phone tighter. I look out the window. I can now see wisps of smoke. *No, not this. Please, not this.*

"Big?" I ask

"Yes."

"We need to leave?" *Please, please say no.*

"Yes."

I inhale, then exhale slowly. *"No…."* It's a cry, an objection.

Our neighbor Dave had just called Ed. Dave was with a group at the camp, fighting a small fire there. A sudden turn of the wind and the fire whipped up, jumped across the camp, and headed our way at full speed. Dave ran to the phone to call us.

The blaze is no longer containable. It is a full-fledged forest fire coming right at us.

It's 6:20 p.m. June 19, 2013.

The Spanish Peaks Scout Ranch is only a mile away. It's above us, so we should be able to take the easy evacuation route, down the road to town.

Inhale. Exhale.

"We need to get out of here," Ed says.

"We'll come up and help you load the horses."

"Ok," he says a little hesitantly. I am afraid of the horses. But I appear to have forgotten that.

I look out the window again. The smoke is building, moving across the pirate's face. Across our mountain.

Joe is at the side door, getting ready to put dinner on the grill.

I look over at him. He has no idea. He's ready to make dinner and enjoy another relaxing evening on the mountain. Unaware, as I was a few happy moments ago.

"Fire at the scout camp," I tell him, repeating Ed, my voice wheezy. I can't quite breathe. "We need to leave."

"Oh, no!" It's a cry, an objection.

We look at one another. I am still glued to the chair, my hands still clutching the phone. *Inhale, exhale, breathe.*

He throws the vegetables onto the table, no longer focused on dinner, and asks. "What should we take?"

We're in problem-solver mode. Calm, in charge. Somber. But I begin to cough—my body's reaction to stress. I take a swig of water and a swig of the bourbon. *Inhale, exhale.* Then focus. *Inhale, exhale.*

I begin to put things on the table for Joe to carry to the car: my computer and cell phone; my drawing supplies, including the pirate sketch; the file case filled with our papers because we knew this could happen; underwear and socks for both of us. And the bottle of cheap bourbon. I don't remember packing the bourbon, but it ends up on my lap in the car and I am glad.

I have just showered and am wearing old sweats. I throw on whatever "town clothes" are closest— ratty jeans, a shirt with a hole in it, socks, and my slip-on hiking shoes—a bad choice I end up wearing for days.

I close the windows, then think maybe you're supposed to leave windows open during a fire. No, that's a tornado. I leave them shut. We run out, close the door behind us, scramble up the path to Mr. Green Jeans, our elderly Toyota 4Runner, and drive up to help Ed and Gwyn. In doing so, we are driving toward the fire. Once they're ready to go we'll turn around and drive back past our cabin, then down the mountain, away from the blaze.

The horses—Czarina and a visitor, Indie, owned by a friend of Gwyn's—climb into the trailer easily, perhaps sensing the danger themselves. Joe helps Gwyn lead them in. The dogs, Ross and Bella, are already in the truck, sitting upright, alert, watching with ears cocked.

"Do you have your medicines?" Gwyn asks me. "And enough clothes for a week or more? People always forget those." Living north of Colorado Springs, she knows about forest fires.

I hadn't really thought of that many clothes or of medicine at all. I start to run back to the cabin to get them.

"Take the car," Ed yells.

Uh, OK. Yeah, the car. I jump back into Mr. Green Jeans and drive off, leaving Joe behind to wonder where the hell I have gone.

I dash into the cabin and grab an armful of jeans and shirts from the middle of the closet, hoping half will be Joe's, half mine. I dump the medicine cabinet into a sack. No time to fetch our suitcases from the shed down the hill. Joe soon comes running after me, too focused on safety to be annoyed about why I had driven off without him.

Smoke is building over the mountain and the air smells like a campfire. Ash floats in front of us, landing on Mr. Green Jeans. And we're out of there. Horses, dogs, people and things loaded, we speed down the road away from the fire, away from the burning mountain.

Gwyn follows us with her Toyota Tundra pulling the horse trailer. We don't see Ed, who should be coming next. Joe says Ed was watering their house the last time he saw him, using a 200-gallon water tank on the back of his 30-year-old Ford 350.

We drive past Jim and Cherie Bryant's house—they live in Texas and have not been able to visit the mountain much lately. As usual, the house is empty. We like them and appreciate having them as neighbors, but we're glad they're not here now. Ash is raining down on their house and a finger of smoke is poking over the ridge behind it. We hurry past.

Joe usually tells me I go too fast on our road and he worries that I'll break an axle or drive off one of the steep banks or run into a tree or get hung up on a rock. This time he lets me go as fast as I can.

"We've talked about this," Joe says. He leans forward in the passenger seat, his hands on his knees ready to bolt. His head jerks, hawk-like, as he glances back, ahead, to the side, then back again, searching for signs of the fire. "But I never thought it would actually happen." The bad stuff always affects other people, so we are never really ready.

But, while I am eager to flee, I am a little worried we are overreacting. That we'll go speeding down the mountain and our neighbors will see us and laugh at the city folks running away from nothing. We make the two miles to Harlan and Pat's ranch quickly. They're our closest full-time neighbors and they are loading their truck, their faces solemn. That's when I know for sure it is real, that we aren't being alarmists. Harlan and Pat are leaving too.

"Where do you plan to go?" Harlan asks when we drive up.

"I don't know," I answer. Never thought of it. I am just getting out.

I look back toward the mountain, toward our cabin. A thick column of smoke reaches into the sky by now, but it is still a white plume, like a cloud. Without Dave's warning, we would not have thought much of it. Without Dave's warning, we would have been in the middle of it.

In recent years residue from fires in Arizona and New Mexico has reached our valley, so even the smell of smoke would not have completely alarmed us. And we find out later that our road is not even on the sheriff's map, so we never would have received a warning call to evacuate.

We continue to the switchback that is the entrance to our valley, a hairpin curve cut into the rocky hillside; this is a private road Harlan built and maintains. We have no guardrails. That used to bother me; now I don't even notice it, although I always slow down there because I am not a complete fool. We make the "u" turn in the road and are now facing the mountain. It is a stew of smoke— orange, black, grey, and yellow. Mean looking.

We can get a cellphone signal on the switchback hill, so I call Phyllis in Pueblo. I know the fire will be on the news soon, and she will worry. We're all fine, I tell her. Oh, and by the way, can we stay with you tonight? Of course, she says. Be safe.

It is 6:47 p.m.

We drive to Fiore and Pearl's at the bottom of the switchback. Fiore, who is 88, grew up on this land. He and his family built their house from logs off the mountain.

Pearl is in the driveway watching the fire build with eyes full of tears and grief.

"The second time," she cries. "The second time." Their entire house burned in the 1950s and she fears that is about to happen again.   We both hug her. Their daughter Melva runs down the steps with an armful of clothes. Fiore is inside their enclosed porch, looking out a window that frames a view of the mountain and their valley. "It's not too bad," he insists. "It'll blow the other way." He is firmly settled in a wooden chair, his wiry rancher's frame upright and steady, his cowboy boots solidly on the ground. It is clear he isn't going anywhere. An oxygen tank sits next to him but is not connected.

We look out the window with him. The wind whips the smoke to the right, then to the left, first clearing up the sky so we can see the mountain clearly, then covering it completely with smoke. Could he be right? Might it blow over? Please make him right, please make it blow over.

I keep my eye on the switchback, waiting for Ed and Gwyn to come down after us, but there is no sign of them. Is Ed still up there, trying to fight this alone?

Fiore has serious lung problems, the extent of which we don't understand until two hospice nurses and a chaplain drive up. "Your lungs are delicate," one nurse tells him gently, kneeling next to him. "We need to get you out of this smoke." He wants to stay put, insisting it is going to go the other way.

The nurses know he has to leave, though, and they help him and Pearl get ready. They search for the numerous oxygen canisters throughout the house and load them. Trying to help, I point out a hose in the corner: "There's one." The nurse looks over, then laughs, touching my arm. "That's actually a vacuum cleaner," she says, "but if you want to tidy up, go ahead." I laugh with her.

I again search the switchback for signs of Ed and Gwyn. The longer we wait, the edgier I get. The fire is moving fast. Did they get caught in it? I busy myself helping take photo albums and boxes out of Pearl and Fiore's house, and getting him his favorite hat.

With tears in his eyes, Fiore agrees to leave.

It's 7:32 p.m. Time to leave the mountain completely. It's been 45 minutes since we left our cabin. What has happened to Ed and Gwyn? They should have been right behind us.

Finally, I remember there is a different route out of our land, that the switchback is not our only exit. Ed and Gwyn have probably taken the other way out. I exhale with relief. We have only been on the other road once—it has five different gates and is an inconvenient drive—so we seldom even think about it being there. Its entrance is tucked away behind a hill past Harlan and Pat's, one of many little dirt paths going here, there, and, often, nowhere. It is easy to miss and to forget.

I choose to believe they went that way, bypassing the switchback, and they are somewhere farther down the road.

We leave and, as we drive toward Interstate 25, we watch the smoke continue to billow. By now it is dark, and we can see glowing neon tongues leaping hundreds of feet high. We drive the 45 minutes to Pueblo in silence as behind us, the red flames rise below the pirate's head, burning over the valley we just left.

5. There Can't Be Anything Left

I call Phyllis as soon as we get to Interstate 25, the minute I can get a decent signal. She says Ed and Gwyn had waited for us on the road for about 45 minutes, then Gwyn went on with the horses, while Ed stayed, looking out for us. He apparently had left only minutes ago, so we are following him down the highway, the glow of the fire at our backs.

Gwyn did not trust her trailer brakes and the horse trailer on the switchback plus it's shorter the way they went if all the gates are open, which they were. *Thank God*, I silently pray, the first of the tears starting. Tears of relief soon give way to shock and grief. Up until now, I have been moving on adrenaline and disbelief. Now, I am beginning to feel.

Joe is now driving, so I send our kids, Josh and Ellen and son-in-law Steve, an email: "Fire at the scout camp. We're on our way to Pueblo. Ed, Gwyn, horses and dogs headed to Monument." I want them to be informed but not alarmed, as they love this land too. Tears roll down my face as I write, and I know they will drip right into our conversation if I call. Better to wait, collect myself, know more.

"Holy moley," Ellen answers, "Be safe. Love you."

"Yikes," Josh writes. "Keep me posted."

"Be safe," Steve writes.

I imagine other people driving by and seeing the flames on the mountain. "Hey, Maude, look at that. I wonder what's there." Maude looks and answers, "Probably nothing much. Should be four more hours to Santa Fe."

I look back as we drive toward Pueblo. The flames do not abate. They are all I can see. Finally, I turn, stare into the dark ahead, and try to connect with myself. But if I don't think about this, if I don't face it, maybe it is not true.

Phyllis meets us at the door, hugs us, and offers us food. We have not eaten—our dinner remains on the cabin table—so we agree to some cheese and crackers and wine. Ironically, she gives us smoked Gouda. I wonder, briefly, if it is situations like this—forest fires—that got people to smoke things in the first place, or to have things smoked for them.

The fire is the lead story on the late-night news. A reporter stands at the La Veta airport, 20 miles away from our land; the fire, smoke, and flames are her backdrop. Nearly 300 acres have burned so far, she says, and the fire is zero percent contained. A few hundred acres sounds manageable. Maybe Fiore was right, and it is not a big deal, it will blow over. Still, some of those 300 acres are likely ours. Most, even. We're all silent. I feel my tears and see Joe's and Phyllis's.

The blasted wind is helping spread the flames. And the dry trees are kindling. Firefighters are already there, with more to come. Helicopters to drop water are expected on Saturday. "Saturday!" we say in unison. Today is Wednesday. That's three days before we get helicopters. But this is the eighth fire burning in Colorado right now, so resources are thin.

The station lists the roads that are closed. County Roads 317, 330, 340. All roads that lead to ours. But they never list ours. We don't exist, yet here we are.

The next morning, we go to a thrift shop in Pueblo to get Joe clothes. Turns out that what I grabbed for him when we evacuated is what he wears when he climbs under the cabin or digs holes or cuts trees. For only $44 we buy him shirts, pants, and pajamas. I borrow a pair of sandals from Phyllis because my clunky hiking boots are hot. My feet are a size bigger than hers, so my heels and toes hang out.

I compliment Joe on his pants and ask their brand.

"Heinz," he says.

"Huh?" I ask.

He begins to laugh. "I meant Dockers," he says. And I laugh with him. Our minds are clogged with smoke stress. Laughing at the nonsense that comes out of our mouths is refreshing.

We decide to drive to the southern tip of Pueblo, where we can see the smoke and assess the fire. Once there, we go a bit farther, then farther, and pretty soon we are in Walsenburg, 15 miles away from the cabin, probably 12 miles from the fire. The smoke gets deeper and darker the closer we get.

Ash drifts softly over the city. When I see people walking down the streets, smoking, I want to slap the cigarettes from their hands. We stop at the high school, which has been set up as a relief center for those evacuated from the fire, to see if any neighbors are there. No. We see several scouts, fellow victims, who scrambled out just ahead of the fire as we did, their own paradise destroyed.

We go to George's Drive Inn because it's a local favorite; maybe somebody there can help us find Pearl and Fiore. We don't know Melva's last name, but we know they were headed to her house northeast of the city. This is a small town and the waitress I talk to went to school with Melva and looks her up in the phone book. I call and am beyond delighted to hear they are OK, that Fiore made the trip fine and both are handling the fire as well as the rest of us, however that is.

We head to Ideal Road, the most direct route to our land, and are surprised there are no barriers there. We drive to a hill overlooking the mountain, about three miles from our switchback. Smoke hides the mountain and burns our eyes. I can see a patch of green where our valley starts. Through the gray and black and orange and red, a little green.

We wait as a car comes along the ridge and down to us. The driver stops and introduces herself as Frank's daughter—Frank and Sue live just past Harlan and Pat. but we seldom see them because we take the switchback and therefore don't go past their house.

We tell her who we are and where we live.

She shakes her head gravely.

"The way the fire burned down the valley, there can't be anything left," she says.

I want to ask about the green, but our places are two miles beyond what I can see, so she might well be right. I don't have the heart to challenge her.

6. In a Forest Fire, Pecan Pie is Often Sadly Overlooked

The photo from Dave is terrifying: a giant explosion in the direction of our homes, taken shortly after we left. A monster orange flame bursting into the black sky. He took it from his home, three crow miles from us. I gasp, blink, look again.

What could it be if not our homes? That's really all that's there that could make such a cataclysm. Our beautiful little mountain homes that we built ourselves with such love and excitement.

I blink again, this time to try to control the tears.

It's June 21, 2013, two days after the fire, and we're with Ed and Gwyn at their home in Monument, two hours away from our land. The air here is also full of smoke and ash from fires burning all over south-central Colorado. Ours is but one in a crowded field of chaos.

I show the photo to Joe. "Ohhhh…." he says.

I show it to Gwyn. "Oh, no," she says, tears welling in her eyes.

I show it to Ed. He says nothing, just sighs.

In the email with the photos, Dave also tells me he and his two brothers and their families are fine. They all live on Bear Creek Road, which parallels our road and ends in the scout camp. Their family actually built the camp on land they own. His brother Doug's house got hit, but firefighters were able to save it. About eight homes around the camp have burned, including Doc's beautiful rock-top pentagon.

Dave asks for a phone number so he can call and tell us what he knows. And, he writes, "I am so happy that all of you are safe, I was so worried that you might not have had enough time to evacuate."

I give him Ed and Gwyn's number. And, by the way, I say, thanks for warning us. You saved our lives. I imagine us still there in that ball of flame, driving by as the house explodes, the blast hitting Mr. Green Jeans, setting him on fire as we bolt into the blackened meadow. I shoo the image away. Reality is enough, I don't need to imagine worse.

Soon Dave calls. Ed puts him on speakerphone. Dave is also in tears. The fire burned so ferociously nothing could have survived, he says. He is at his sister's in Canon City and will return as soon as it is safe. We have nothing to contribute, and the conversation is short and unspeakably sad.

Ed hangs up. We're all in silent, shocked mourning. Gwyn leaves the room quietly sobbing.

We have spent the last two days looking at maps online showing where the fire burned. We pinpointed our homes: The fire was right there. And there. And there. Even before Dave called, we were sure we had lost it all. Steve helped us coordinate Google Earth with the Forest Service maps that showed burn areas marked "isolated heat source," "intense heat," and "scattered heat sources." The intense heat is clearly on the ridges, the scattered heat higher on the mountain. All around our homes, though, are isolated heat sources. What the devil are isolated heat sources? We figure they must be trees. Or, of course, houses.

"Fingers continue to be crossed," Steve writes.

On Facebook, Josh and Ellen keep friends updated on what they both call Our Beloved Cabin.

"I am heartbroken, and I know you are too," Ellen emails me. I am, honey, I am.

Family members throughout the country are checking in via social media for news. "I can't think of anything else," our niece in Memphis writes in an email.

A member of our church in Iowa asks exactly where our cabin is on the Forest Service map, as he and his wife have been tracking online. Our insurance agent calls and opens a claim.

We hear that actor James Gandolfini has died. I imagine him on our deck. He is smoking a cigar because, at this point, why not?

I comment on Facebook whenever I know something and try to remain hopeful but that's getting to be a chore.

We Skype with Ellen and Josh, which is a tonic. They make me laugh; they comfort me. Bless their dear hearts. They both know that the loss of the land is like the loss of a friend, even if we are all fine ourselves. Their hearts are right where mine is.

Then Harlan calls. And in an instant, things change. "Oh, your places are just fine! I've just been up there to see them," he says in his no-nonsense, pay-attention-and-quit-being-silly way. "There's a few little fires between the cabin and the cottage that you should come up and put out."

We whiplash from tears to laughter. Our cabin is fine. Ed and Gwyn's little ranch is fine.

The huge plume Dave had photographed was our neighbor's, the Bryant's, home. I remember driving by it and seeing the smoke rising behind it. It's gone, Harlan says. We're silent at that news. Like us, Jim and Cherie love this place. We're all shaken for them, but so very glad they were not there.

Harlan and Pat are already back on the mountain and their house is safe. Pearl and Fiore's house also remains untouched.

And now Harlan says we should go up and put out some little fires. Little? How little? Put them out? How?

At this point, what is now officially called the East Peak Fire has burned about 8,000 of its ultimate 13,500 acres. It is moving fast, fueled by continued high winds. Fire fighters from all over the country are there. So we're supposed to go to help them? With, apparently, buckets and towels, according to Harlan. Seriously? Hundreds of people have been evacuated from the mountain, foothills, and even some of the high desert between the peak and Walsenburg. No one is officially allowed back in.

But Ed and Joe do go up—with no hesitation. We load them with food and water, and they jump into Ed's Ford 350 and are off for the two-hour drive from Monument to Walsenburg. Ed calls when they get there. No barricades block the road yet, so they get right in and are surprised to find a full complement of fire fighters on our little road—a small pump truck and two pickups, each with three fire fighters.

They have come from all over, part of a squadron of 519 professionals assigned to the fire. The head of the fire-fighting team is from the South Dakota Division of Wildland Fire. They're backed by five helicopters, 36 fire engines, 16 water tenders, and three bulldozers. The Colorado Army National Guard and the Colorado Air National Guard are also providing firefighting, security, and communication help. A water truck is parked at Harlan and Pat's for refueling. Helicopters scoop water from Bear Lake, on the ridge above Ed and Gwyn's.

The next morning, Joe calls and tells me he and Ed spent a long afternoon and evening filling up buckets, soaking towels, and throwing them on smoldering fires, keeping them from spreading and becoming worse. But the smoke is heavy, he has a headache, and he would like to leave.

Phyllis and I drive back to the mountain intending to pick him up, hoping we can also convince Ed to leave and to not return until the fire is contained. Ed says he's staying, though.

It seems that all of Colorado is on fire. Even though Mr. Green Jeans has been parked in Pueblo, 50 miles north of the peak, it's covered with ash, but that is from a different fire to the west, near Wolf Creek Pass. The drive from Pueblo to Walsenburg is hazy. As we near the East Spanish Peak, the thick smoke blows from the mountain toward the east.

Our mountain is on fire. I keep repeating this to myself. I now finally understand the concept of surreal.

We stop in Walsenburg and get a pecan pie. Phyllis doesn't believe she can go up to see Ed without bringing something. She always brings something. Manners don't go out the window just because the smoke has come in. We also get ice cream. In the rulebook of how to behave in a forest fire, bringing pecan pie and ice cream is often sadly overlooked.

·   ·   ·

We take our usual route from Walsenburg, up Ideal Road next to the cemetery and alongside the train tracks, ready to drive the 14 miles up to our land.

Or maybe not.

The National Guard now blocks the road. One Humvee and two guards in fatigues. We stop, and a guardsman comes up to us. I roll down the window to talk. He has a list of people who are allowed in, people with animals. I say I have no livestock, but I do have a husband who needs tending. That doesn't fly. I can go up to feed my chickens, but not get my husband out. This is ranching country—husbands should be able to take care of themselves. Livestock can't.

We try another route, along Bear Creek Road. The guard there seems amenable to our going in and makes a call on his walkie-talkie. Turns out he is calling the guard at the other road who says, "Yeah, she was just here."

Oh, good, now I have a record.

A sheriff's deputy comes to the car with a map, asking where Joe is. I try to show him, but our road is not even on his map. He has an updated version of a Huerfano County map, and our road is gone. It has been there in previous versions. Good heavens, have we been burned right off the map? I show him where we should be, and he says he'll send somebody up. A few minutes later, I decide I will find a way in, so I tell him Joe is coming down on his own. He calls off the deputy. I'll figure something else out.

A convoy is leaving the sheriff's office at 1:30 p.m. with people who need to go up to feed livestock; we'll do that. I will invent some chickens. After a quick lunch of ice cream in a Walsenburg park, Phyllis and I go to stand in line and wait for the sheriff.

We meet Dave there and he goes up with us. Nobody asks what kind of livestock we have, so I do not have to lie.

We are the sixth car in a convoy of 12 and we drive down the gravel road toward the smoke. One by one, the others turn off at their houses and ranches and at side roads until it is just us in Mr. Green Jeans. The fire is burning strongest to the east of us. It's covered three valleys so far and the ridges in between. But right now, it is doing its damage elsewhere.

Dave continues a nervous chatter in the back seat, probably to keep our minds off what we are doing, probably to keep his own mind off what we are doing. He explains that burned trees are still usable as lumber, because only the outer layer burns, leaving green wood inside. But, he says, working with them is a mess, as the ash gets all over your clothes and skin.

We turn on our road, climb up the ridge, and curve toward the mountain. We don't take the switchback, as Ed says that could be blocked by fire crews. We're on the gentler slope that starts toward the east then turns south, facing the mountain. The road that Ed and Gwyn had taken out, the road we forgot existed.

If I were to make a movie about hell, this would be how I would portray it. Grey, everything is grey. Even what remains green has a grayish film. To our left is a wall of smoke—amber, orange, blue, slate. Smaller funnels of blue grey smoke burst throughout the valley and over the hillsides and up the mountain. Ashen plumes rise, dissipate, rise again, moving gently east with the wind. The pirate formation is a mass of smoke; we can see flames on the pirate's pine beard.

Hot embers line the narrow roadside.

"I wouldn't drive on those," Dave says.

"Fair enough," I agree.

Phyllis is silent, but I can feel her nerves; if I don't drive straight enough for her, she leans over and grabs the wheel to keep the car safely off the coals.

A group of firefighters comes down the road toward us in a pickup and drives up on the bank so we can get through; they are leaving. They're from Vail, Colorado. I ask them about going up. "You'll be fine right now," they say. "The wind has settled." I choke up as I weepily thank them for all they have done.

They look away, embarrassed.

We continue our drive. Soon we end up behind another fire truck, crawling up slowly, looking for fires along the way. The truck stops, and I go up to talk to the driver.

"Do you want to go past us?" he asks. "Absolutely not," I say. Nothing safer when driving through a forest fire than following the fire truck.

After about a half hour on our road, we get to the Bryants' and slowly, silently drive by. What had been a two-story log home is now only a concrete foundation and a twisted metal roof. Everything flattened. I barely want to look. Ironically, even though the house is destroyed, many of the surrounding trees still stand. Thankfully, Dave warned us to get out the night of the fire, as the Bryants' explosion would have blocked our escape had we been only a few minutes later. Or we could have been caught right in it.

Beyond the Bryants' we pass the shed in which we had stored our junk. No sign of the shed itself, only the deformed frame of our old futon, two chipped porcelain sinks, a metal stove perfectly intact.

Then to our little cabin, which is beautifully, miraculously, and happily fine. Our little place absolutely like a dear friend right now. The path to it is singed, nearby scrub oaks are burned, the grass brown. Our outhouse, about 20 feet from the cabin, has been vaporized. Nothing remains, not even an ash footprint.

Our grill with its gas cylinder is out in the meadow, along with our deck furniture and two deck rugs, moved there by the firefighters to protect the house.

Smoke rises in pockets on the far ridge across the meadow. Fine bits of ash float in the air. I look toward the mountain and watch what's left of the pirate smolder.

I try not to think about any of it. I am here to get Joe. While I wait for him, I go back in to pack more things in case the fire doubles back. Joe comes down the road—he had been up on higher ground trying to call me. I had tried to call him as well, but neither of us had a signal. He is annoyed with me because he didn't know when I was coming, and I therefore am annoyed with him. I got here, didn't I? I came to pick you up in a dad-blasted forest fire, so give me a break. We're both dealing with a level of stress for which we could never have prepared, so this is less annoyance and more worry, concern for one another and for ourselves, our neighbors, and the mountain. The beautiful mountain.

Joe has already gotten things ready to go, and I pick up more. Phyllis and Dave go up to find Ed and try to talk him into leaving. No dice. He is staying. He does take the pie, though.

Later, Ed tells me I was a basket case. I disagree, saying I thought I was relatively calm. I felt relatively calm, in the context of a person in the middle of a forest fire. Granted, the fire itself was calm right then, which helped my state of mind, but I knew it could change.

As we're standing in the road, gathering our things and our wits, a fire truck comes up from the right. Within minutes, another one comes from the left. We're penned in by fire trucks. This is a two-mile long, rutty road with only three houses on it and one of them is already gone. I had not thought we would get this level of personal attention. Still, the fire started a mile away, so we are in the midst of it, and preserving our houses keeps the fire from spreading. At least that is my justification for these men risking so much for my little patch of earth and its sweet little cabin.

The chief of this crew gets out of the driver's side of one truck and Harlan gets out of the other side. It is weeks later before we learn that the first trucks only came up here to tend our houses in the first place because of Harlan. They hadn't known we were there until he told them.

Without our neighbors and the firefighters, we feel sure we would not have had anything left.

"You left in a hurry the other night," the chief kids us. "Your dinner was still on the table."

"Yep," we agree.

"Well, we went in and shut your windows," he says. Then, laughing: "But we didn't wash your dishes." I remember shutting the windows, but then realize I forgot the windows in the kitchen and bathroom. Forgot they even existed.

"I guess we'll have to come back for the dishes later," I say, attempting to smile winningly, but probably just looking goofy.

"They'll keep," the chief says, putting a comforting hand on my shoulder.

"They will," I say. I force my voice not to shake, but I feel the tears coming, so I pull out the keys and busy myself with opening the car door.

We all thank the chief and Harlan multiple times and then they get back into their truck with the chief driving. He expertly turns around in the narrow tree-lined road and drives off to check a fire in the meadow. The other fire truck goes to another fire in a nearby grove of scrub oak. Phyllis, Dave, Joe, and I drive down the mountain, back through hell.

Phyllis is distraught that Ed will not come with us, but glad he at least took the pie, which he shares with the firefighters.

At the end of Ideal Road, we check in with the National Guard, so they can take us off the list of people who are up on the mountain. "You got him," the guard says to me, nodding at Joe in the back seat.

"Moo," Joe says.

It is 3:45 p.m. June 22.

We stop in Walsenburg to get gas and see a local television crew hanging around. They ask if we live nearby. We say we do, and they want to interview us. I agree, taking the opportunity to thank the firefighters and Dave. Afterward, I realize I am still wearing the same old shirt and ratty jeans I threw on when we evacuated. My hair has not seen a comb in quite a while.

I mention all this to Phyllis.

"Plus, you have a hole in your blouse," she says, pointing to a sizable tear on my collar. Ever the helpful older sister.

Oh well.

I never do see that newscast. My nephew Dan says I did a good job, but he loves me. Still I got my message out: Thank you.

We think the fire has calmed, maybe even ended, but Ed calls that night to tell us differently. After we left, he watched the wind gradually build again. The fire chief came by and together they watched a new blaze grow on and spread across the meadow, toward the road out.

"Does that worry you?" Ed asked.

"No," the chief said, "but that does." He pointed behind Ed. The fire had spiked again by the scout camp.

"Should I leave?" Ed asked.

"We will when you do," the chief answered.

It was 6 p.m. June 22. Almost three days since the fire started.

Ed left, and the fire burned back on itself, coming again to the valley, back toward the meadow, back to where we thought all was well. Ed, Harlan, and the firefighters stood on the road, looking back at thick black smoke that was thousands of feet above the peak, listening to the roar that sounded like an approaching train, the growl of the wind rushing toward them snorting fire.

7. We Feel Like Cowards. We Feel Sane

Once again, we're with Ed and Gwyn, waiting for news of the fire. Ed's face is pale with grief, his eyes bloodshot. He had gone back into the fire and tried to save what he could, and now he sits with us, quietly brooding.

We try to call Harlan multiple times for his update but get no answer. The phone service has been cut off from the burn area, and cell phones have never been reliable there. We check online and the fire news remains grim. By now, it has claimed 13,000 acres.

Air tankers dropped 46,000 gallons of retardant on the fire shortly after Ed left, which slowed the inferno he'd seen. Much of it ended up on land adjoining ours; some ended on ours. Ed says that, without that drop, our houses would have burned.

Blessedly, nobody has been hurt.

It's June 23, 2013, five days after the fire started.

I call the information number for the East Peak Fire. I expect a recording, but a woman answers. She tells me where the fire is contained and where the firefighters are building barriers to keep it from spreading. I check her information with my map and see that they are on the mountain itself, above our land. I am not sure if this is good news or not.

"Ask about loss of structures," Ed suggests.

"No structures have been lost since Thursday," the woman answers. That is the day after the fire. We had returned on Friday. We're OK again. OK still. OK perhaps. We think. We hope. We really have no idea.

Ed is going up, no matter what. We pack food he can eat if there are no kitchens left.

Joe and I decide to head back to Iowa for a respite. Away from the constant smoke of Southern Colorado that makes it difficult to breathe. This is no place for a person with emphysema, but I don't even think about that until later. I'll be back as soon as I can; my concern is what is happening to our land; my lungs don't enter into the equation at all.

A Facebook friend in Denver offers us a room at her house. A former student offers her parent's house in Nebraska. Steve finds cheapish tickets to Vermont. But we head to Iowa instead; it's simpler. Neighbors greet us with homemade ginger snaps and a pitcher of hard lemonade and help us finish it off, listening to our ranting about the fire like the good women they are.

We plan to come back when we know what is happening. Maybe we'll come back to a cabin, maybe to bare land. But we'll come back. We feel like cowards, heading east, away from it all. We feel sane.

We're almost at the Nebraska border when Gwyn calls us, laughing happily. All our structures are safe. Ed is in his mountain home and plans to stay there for the duration. When residents are officially allowed in, she will go back with the horses. Harlan and Pat are home for good. So are Fiore and Pearl.

Much of our forest is gone, but at least our homes are fine.

We both exhale, perhaps for the first time in days.

"Well, thank God," I say.

"Yes," Joe says. "Yes."

•   •   •

On July 1, ten days after the fire started, Gwyn moves back. We return a week later.

We see the first signs of the aftermath about five miles from the cabin, as we go over a hill on Ideal Road. This is usually one of my favorite views, one that often pops up in my mind when I am not thinking of anything else, the dreamlike image that is sort of the wallpaper for my subconscious. The entire mountain fills the view, from east to west, with the foothills lapping at the bottom. Now those hills are black, with charcoal fingers of burned trees all the way up the mountain to tree line. An oval of burned trees at the bowl must be where the miner's cabin had been.

The mountain is wounded.

We retrace our steps, stopping first at Fiore and Pearl's. Their comfortable log house is untouched; they're in the kitchen and invite us in to chat. The hillside behind their house is seared; the fire came a few hundred yards from them, into a meadow that is home to elk and the bears that often raid their chicken coop. Fiore seems livelier than we have seen him in a while; returning home—having a home to return to—has been good for him. Pearl offers iced tea, as she always does, but we are anxious to get to the cabin, so we don't stay long.

We drive up the switchback and wordlessly look at one seared hillside after another. The road has been widened a bit by the firefighters, a few trees cut so they could get through.

We pull up before Harlan and Pat's. The hill behind their alfalfa meadow is a total burn; ahead of us, on the road, we can see patches of green and patches of black. Their house is also unblemished, but the fire came frighteningly close to the back of it. Had Frank not shown up the night of the fire with his bulldozer, and had firefighters not continued to fight the blaze, they feel their house would have been gone.

This is the theme: Neighbors helped neighbors, and the firefighters helped us all. Again, our visit is short. We're anxious.

The two-mile drive to the cabin is both heartening and heartbreaking. Much green remains. Much of what had been green is black. The side of the road is lined with what looks like charcoal briquettes, shrubs are now just black sticks, the rocks are singed. Yet many of the trees rimming the road are gorgeous and alive. As we look higher up the hill, though, all is black and deathly gray. Huge swathes of forest are now charred fields with skeletal trees poking up from an ash floor.

We drive by the Bryants' again, shuddering at its total destruction. Then to the cabin. It feels so normal to walk inside. Other than being a little messy, it looks the way it always has—sweet and welcoming. Thanks to the firefighters, there is no smell of smoke. Thanks to Ed, there is no food smell. After the fire, he came and cleaned out our refrigerator, threw out the spoiled food, mixing it in with their manure pile, and washed our dishes. God love him.

Before we can shower, Joe has to clean ash out of our water heater vent. He has to do this several times before we finally get a new water heater.

Our cabin is fine. Our mountain is not. At times I wish it were the other way around, as the cabin would be easier to rebuild than the mountain. I get over that quickly, because the cabin is our handiwork, and, in many ways, is us.

Fourteen structures were lost in the fire, mostly near the scout camp, but the burn was erratic. A veterinarian who lived at least two miles east of the camp lost his house, outbuildings, and equipment. Neighbors even farther away lost a historic barn, built more than 100 years ago. The damage generally happened early, before firefighters came on the scene. Most important: All the firefighters are safe, and all the residents got out in time.

Thousands of acres in the San Isabel National Forest and on neighboring land on all sides of us are burned. The final tally for the East Peak fire is just over 13,500 acres. About half our land is burned.

Fire is good for grass, however, and the meadow looks good, except for yellowed patches of trails left by the fire trucks.

Significant destruction struck when the fire rekindled to our west and roared back through, after I came to pick up Joe. I had taken photos of the meadow and hillsides on that visit; all the trees were green except for those at the top of the ridge. Now, about a quarter of those along the hillside are gone or damaged so much they are not likely to make it.

This is like watching a loved one go through a devastating illness. Our mountain does not deserve this, and we feel its pain.

8. Walking Sideways

We're eating dinner on the deck, martinis in hand. This is cherished time here, time to relax and watch for wildlife, usually across the meadow on the Bear Highway, our name for the animal trail that skirts the opposite ridge, running through groves of scrub oak and fields of grass. It's a well-worn footpath, created by decades of bears, deer, and elk traipsing this way and that in search of food, water, and mates.

If we don't look too closely, the view is normal—stately firs and pines and spruces reach from the meadow toward the sky in green splendor. But tucked in between them are patches of rust and charcoal. At the top, the ridge is black. Total burn. So we don't look too closely.

We hear a shuffling, then see a movement in front of us, a shape on the boulder less than five feet from us. A furry foot is reaching from the rock to the deck. A big furry foot attached to a bear. Seems he's planning on coming onto the deck.

"Shoo!" I shout. Seriously, this works on black bears. He probably weighs three times as much as me, even though he is small—he looks like he is only a year or two old. Still, he runs away when I yell at him. He trundles up the hill toward the shed then stops, turns, and looks at me, wondering if I am serious. "Shoo!" I shout again, clapping my hands. This time he lumbers all the way to the road. He stays there and watches us. I yell at him again. He stays put.

He's the mangy fellow who has invited himself to be our neighbor, moving in within throwing distance of the cabin, in a cove of trees that dips into the creek. His coat is dirty beige and looks like the stuffing from a 100-year-old mattress. But he usually leaves us alone. When we work outside, he calmly grazes in the grass just yards away from us, barely paying attention to us. Until now, we've not appeared to be worth his time.

I shout at him again. "Get out of here!" He looks at me. Shrugs. "Shoo! Get!" He finally bumbles down the road, his ratty butt swaying with each step.

We begin to lock the door at night, a first, but extra insurance in case he tries to get in. Bears have been known to turn door handles, especially the lever style we have on our screen door. We leave our windows open about two inches, hoping that's too small an opening to lure him although it's enough to give him a foothold should he seriously want to break in. We leave no food out anywhere.

It's mid-July, two weeks since we returned, and animals are hungry; much of their food sources burned. Bears are omnivores, eating nuts, berries, fruits, grasses, squirrels, mice, and insects such as ants and wasps. We usually know a bear is around when we find holes dug into anthills, or rocks turned over in search of insects or rodents. Or poop full of berries. Unbelievable that something so big can feast on such miniscule food. Bears can roam more than 100 miles in search of food, so we wonder why so many are hanging around here, with such a small patch of green. Perhaps they also are in shock.

Before the fire, we often saw a mama bear and her two cubs on the Bear Highway, mama working at finding food and the babies frolicking next to her, stumbling up the hill and tumbling down in little rolling mounds of fur. We're heartened when we see all three again. They survived. Often, mama and the babies graze peacefully in the grass, finding sustenance in something that is growing there, probably roots. When they're not around, we search the area and see nothing edible. But we're not bears.

We have an empty trashcan on our back deck in which I put an old pair of hiking boots, planning to take them to the shelter in town. Night after night, a bear gets into the can, chews on the boots, then leaves, apparently realizing that they're hard as shoe leather. We finally get a clue and move the can, putting it behind the shed until we go to town. Eventually one boot disappears; we never find it. Hard to imagine any nutrition there, but it would fill an empty stomach.

These are black bears, and despite their name, they can also be brown, red, blond, beige, or a mixture. Mama is reddish; one baby is black, another brown.

Mr. Mangy is a matted blond. Several years ago, we saw two bears mating on the Bear Highway. It took us a bit to figure out why the bear we were watching through our binoculars was two different colors—brown in front and blond in back—and why it was moving so strangely in the grass. We finally comprehended that we were looking at two bears. The act itself took quite a while, so I hope it was good for both of them. I often worry about female animals—do they really want this particular bloke?

Black bears are typically solitary animals, hooking up just for sex and childcare. Mom has primary childcare duty, but dad occasionally helps out by scaring other animals away from the cubs.

They are usually not a problem unless provoked or enticed with food. We are ever mindful that they were here first. And that they are lots bigger and have long claws at the end of strong, giant feet. Plus, teeth.

Neighbors have similar issues with bears, or with being humans in bear country after it has lost much of its natural food supply. Dave forgets to shut his kitchen window and leaves food on his counter after returning from a shopping trip—unusual for a man who grew up here, but indicative of the mental fog we're all in. Hearing noises that night, he assumes it's his sister Debbie, who is visiting. He walks into the kitchen and finds a 250-pound bear chewing on his Rice Krispy treats. She's already eaten all the bread and a bag of protein powder and chewed holes in some empty pop and beer cans.

Dave shouts and claps and the bear dives back out the window she came in. So Dave also is now more careful about his windows and about food on his counters. He names the bear Debbie and wonders how she feels after slurping all that protein powder. I hope not to find out. A buzzed bear sounds like nobody's friend.

In town one day, we talk to Mike, of Mike's Coffee Barn, where I go when I need decent Wi-Fi. Mike is retired military and he started the coffee shop as extra income. His wife owns the yarn shop next door. I saw him the day the sheriff allowed us up to feed animals and rescue husbands during the fire, so I ask about his livestock.

"Our chickens survived," he says. He explains that he and his wife set up an automated watering system so their hens were taken care of while Mike and his wife had to evacuate, and when they returned after the fire the chickens were hale and healthy. Joe and I are pleased with the apparent happy ending until Mike adds:

"And then a bear broke in and ate every single one."

I look at Mike. He just looks back.

"Oh, I'm so sorry," I offer weakly.

He shrugs and shakes his head.

I sigh. What more is there to say? "I'm sorry," I repeat, then take my coffee, walk to my table, and hide my face in my computer.

. . .

Harlan and Pat just bought another home in Oklahoma, a place to go for the winter and, perhaps, in case of another disaster here. They head there for a few days for a family gathering and we offer to water their garden. I love walking to their house because it comes with a beautiful view of the meadow and the high desert beyond—plus it's downhill the entire two miles. I head there one evening and Joe plans to come in the car about a half hour later to drive me home. At one time I would have walked both ways, but my breathing is increasingly difficult because even the slightest breeze blows ash into my lungs.

About halfway there I hear what sounds like a chain saw. I briefly wonder who is cutting, and where. I stop, listen more carefully. That's not a machine. But what? Then I see the shapes in the meadow, under the willows and scrub oak alongside the creek: at least 70 elk, from giant majestic bucks to wee babies. The racket is coming from several of the biggest animals chewing on the trees. I'm awed at the level of the noise: a thudding background tempo of *crunch, crunch,*

crunch. Elk typically eat grass, shrubs, and tree bark, but if they are hungry enough, they'll eat the whole tree. These guys must be hungry.

I back up a few steps, eying the herd. This could be a problem. That's a lot of big animals. I turn partially around, one foot going forward, the other going back, ready to run whichever direction I need. Or I could just jump into the ditch on the side of the road.

Then a slow rumble shakes the ground, turns louder, and becomes a thunder—the elk are stampeding. Headed by the biggest bulls, the entire herd charges. I'm rooted in my spot on the road, too stunned to move, to think.

But they charge the other way, up the meadow and across the road ahead of me. As I watch them scatter, I blow air in short puffs, as though I'm in childbirth, to calm me and to remind me to breathe. Looks like I will not get trampled today.

Even in my fear, I appreciate the magnificence of these beasts—dark stately heads, long, graceful legs, bone-colored antlers the size of a small tree. They're literally as big as a horse, and they're wild, so I am relieved when they disappear up the ridge through the locusts and scrub oak.

I wait until I no longer hear hoofbeats, then I return to my walk, past the spot that had been loaded with elk just moments before, moving slowly, tentatively at first, then a bit faster and finally at normal speed.

Far off, on the other side of the meadow stands a skinny, gawky coyote who had probably been looking hungrily at some of the elk babies. I do not like or trust coyotes, especially if they look emaciated like this one. We've seen them surround deer, skulking and ready to pounce. And we've seen the carnage afterward. This one stays put, although he keeps his eyes on me as I walk. I keep eying him nervously, but eventually I have to turn my back to him. I feel his eyes and regularly turn around to make sure he's not following me. They have never attacked a person up here, but this one feels dangerous, or maybe it's just the fire that's made me see risk I'd not considered before.

Joe comes down the road in Mr. Green Jeans. Certainly, that will scare the coyote away. He stops and asks if I want a ride.

"I'll walk the rest of the way," I say. I can see Harlan and Pat's outbuildings less than a half a mile ahead. By the time I get there, Joe has started the watering, so I sit on the wall and wait. The burned ridge across the alfalfa field looks like a box of charcoal sticks.

The eagles and hawks, once so plentiful, are gone. Even the groups of turkey vultures have disappeared. We see a lone one occasionally, but not the 10 or more that used to cruise on currents of warm air above the ridge.

I hope the birds got out and headed somewhere greener. But what about their fledglings? The fire started in early summer, when babies could still be in the nest.

It's been a rough year for animals—even livestock have also had their trauma. Fiore and Pearl's grandson saved all the cows that had been on land near us, a challenge with animals too confused to move away as the fire literally nipped at them. Local ranchers had to find somewhere else for their herds. Many simply sold them, often at a loss.

One neighbor couldn't get her horses out in time, so they were here while fire burned around them. Although they survived, one was so stressed by the ordeal that, for weeks afterward, she walked sideways and rammed her head constantly against the barn. They finally moved her off the mountain and she improved.

As I watch Joe water on this calm July evening, I think of what that horse went through just a bit more than a month ago on what had also been a tranquil day, of the sudden rush of flames, the overwhelming heat of a fire fueled by a mountain's worth of dry wood. The suddenness of it, the loss of safety in an instant. The confusion and terror.

Imagine being surrounded by that inferno, with no idea where you might be safe, where it might burn next, when you might die. The aluminum markers we had on our trees to mark new trails melted down in the fire. Aluminum melts at 1,221 degrees. Heat at that level is incomprehensible.

My stomach constricts, my shoulders tense, and my arms begin to shake as I'm once again in the middle of the inferno.

I look around at the dead trees, then at Harlan and Pat's comfortable home, and the arc of water as Joe tends their garden.

Over there: destruction. Over here: safety. All random. What can I trust, and how? I'm beginning to feel like that horse. I think I am going forward, but I am actually walking sideways.

9. A Voluptuous Land

S tripped down to its basic elements, the land remains a beauty. Somber but voluptuous. We can see shape and form that had once been hidden by grass and leaves and needles. Ridges are starker, the earth rising in a clearly outlined dome. The trees are geometric, like a Mondrian painting: thick vertical stumps intersected with straight horizontal branches, painted in charcoal, with ashen highlights. And above, the azure Colorado sky.

Billows of smoke pop up occasionally near the tree line on the face of the mountain, like self-contained tornadoes that build, swirl, then disappear. The first time I saw one I thought the fire was restarting and that I should call the forest service, but Pat tells me that's just what the mountain does now; they're the residual effects of the fire. The fire is still burning underground. After a few weeks, they stop.

Our forest has more than five miles of continuous burn, of land stripped of its trees, ripe for even more damage should we get the kinds of rains that have been dogging Colorado Springs after fires there—downpours that flood basements, knock historic homes off their foundations, and close major roads over and over throughout the summer.

We estimate at least 70 percent of our trees are destroyed, but some of those on the edges of the burn area are a mix of green and rust. We're not sure how many of those will make it. I talk to officials at the USDA Natural Resource Conservation Service and at the Colorado State Forest Service. They tell me that trees with some green remaining have a chance, but there's no guarantee. Different people offer different perspectives on how much green means a tree will live, ranging from 30 to 60 percent. It depends on multiple factors, including the type of tree, how big it is, and what part of the tree burned. They all warn that some trees that look healthy this year could be dead next. It is all about shock. Trees, like people, don't always show their stress outwardly, and the effects of trauma can take a while to build. We see that in coming years as every living thing on the mountain tries to adjust, including us.

We know it's time to take our first stab at erosion control. We've had several wonderful rains—as much as an inch a day, which is bounteous for us. We're ecstatic that the remaining trees and grass are getting much-needed moisture.

But it's clear that we have several trouble spots. When a fire burns extremely hot, the combustion of vegetation creates a waxy, water-resistant cover over the soil. The foresters' technical name for this: hydrophobic soils, which literally means soils that are afraid of water. Water cannot soak into this soil; it can only run off.

Plus, with no vegetation to stop it, even a little bit of water can move and build and crush.

Our nephew Russ, Phyllis's son, comes up for a long weekend to help us. He's done his erosion homework, so he guides our process. Russ has helped build all our structures and has been committed to maintenance of our land, so his handiwork is everywhere on the mountain. He is our most frequent visitor and we all look forward to our time with him; he's pleasant, easy company. And he always brings a lot of food, especially good beer and dessert. And a good back, something on short supply here.

We move rocks and downed trees into the likely path of the water, to slow it down. We plan to do more intense work later, but we do not have a sense of urgency, as having too much water sounds more like a dream than a nightmare. We don't yet fully comprehend how the mountain has changed.

We also scatter pinecones. That's how evergreens propagate naturally, but the cones on the ridge were burned along with their trees, so they need a little help from their friends. We gather extras from our meadow and Russ brings some from Phyllis's yard in Pueblo; we throw them carefully at random. It seems a little step, tiny pinecones to rebuild a giant forest, but everything starts with some sort of a seed. We later learn that this only works if the pinecones are new and their seeds still tucked tightly inside. Most of those we used were open and probably empty, so we accomplished little to nothing.

Oh well.

The next day, Russ wants to see how the scout camp looks, so with apprehension and curiosity, we gather hiking sticks, Camelbacks, and water bottles and head out.

Ross and Bella lead the way as they do on most hikes—running ahead of us, up the ridge, across the meadow, chasing wild turkeys, splashing in the creek, occasionally sending bears up a tree. Ross is a mix of lab, bloodhound, and who knows what else, and from toe to ear he's 30 inches tall. Gwyn took him in as a rescue dog, fell in love, and kept him. He's a highly lovable lug—he always greets us with the enthusiasm that comes only from pooches. Occasionally, though, we run into him in the woods and I have a mini heart attack, because he is dark brown and the size of a small bear and he is running through the trees right at me. He's a mountain kind of guy and fits right in up here. That has its lovely side and its pretty icky one. We've seen him eat entire squirrels in one bite, gulping them down with the tail wiggling frantically out of his closed mouth. This is nature. You just get used to it.

Bella is a little black beauty, the adorable runt of the litter, a typical lab in all but size; at 50 pounds, she is on the low end of the scale. Ed calls her Little Darling, and she is a sweetie, although she often would prefer to just settle in for a long nap than go for a walk.

We're a gang of stitched-together seniors hiking the Rockies. The mountain is like family to us and being together on it is like being in the lap of the best grandmother ever.

Russ, at 53, is the youngster. He's no longer biking and hiking like he had been, but he's solid and energetic.

Joe, 75, is the oldest. He's had a heart valve replaced and has weathered prostate cancer, but he hikes like a sonofagun, especially given that he was raised in the Iowa flatlands. People who don't see him in action don't get that such a wiry guy can be so strong.

Ed is 70. He went about a decade too long before he got hip surgery and hiked strenuously for all those years on some bad bones. Surgery helped, and he is out with us again, although he has lingering problems with nerves in his back. He gets steroids regularly—you know he's ready for a shot when his face becomes a mask of pain and he walks in small steps. Today, though, he's walking with only a slight limp.

Gwyn, 66, only has 50 percent of her lung function because of asthma, but she has effective drugs and she often leaves me in the dust. She has iron strong legs. She too has serious back pain, but she takes a pain pill before we head out. She and I deeply regret our chatty breaks together when we were young mothers and headed to a restaurant to smoke so we'd only make ourselves sick and not our kids. And we did make ourselves sick.

I am 67 and the slowest of the bunch. I have an unusual case of emphysema—it hasn't gotten any worse in 20 years even though it's typically a progressive disease. Multiple docs insist I have it, and tests supposedly prove it, but I don't feel like I fit the mold of the standard COPD patient. Maybe it's because I keep active like this. Hiking at 8,000 feet is a challenge for me, but I am going to continue until I am so slow I go backwards. The breast cancer I had seven years ago was treated and is gone.

We walk up the road toward the mountain, through the gate by Ed and Gwyn's outhouse, and then up the hill to our northern ridge, an 85-foot incline, almost 10 stories in an average home. Ed leaves us at the top, going the other direction along the ridge, back to our land to work more erosion control. He has already gone on a long walk today with the dogs.

That small trek takes us from a color photo to a black and white, from our verdant meadow to a giant burn scar. But we've become accustomed to the grim tableau that greets us on top. Much of the time in those first weeks I feel a little vague emotionally—I think I don't want to give in to the sharpness, as it would slice my heart. I just try to keep busy and not think about it too much.

Gwyn says the woods have an eerie beauty now. That's a healthy way of looking at it. They, in fact, are photogenic, with stark angles in shades of grey.

The scout ranch is on 480 acres of land northwest of us. A straight walk there would be a mile each way, but you can't go straight in the mountains, although it is easier now, with fewer trees in the way.

Our view has certainly opened up. We can see the East Peak peering at us on one side and Greenhorn Mountain, 40 miles away, on the other. We normally can barely see in front of us because the rest of the view is hidden behind a fan of greenery.

We look for leftover signs of old trails—indentations in the ground made by decades of animal and human feet, and follow them as much as we can, as they are our link to life before the fire. But often there's nothing left. The familiar markers—the pines, fir, aspens, spruces—are gone and their comfort and clarity gone with them.

After walking half a mile along the ridge, we take the road that drops down into the scout camp's valley. We walk past burned trees marked with orange surveyor's tape. This land belongs to Dave and his family, so we figure that he and his brothers are marking trees to cut. We wonder why they selected some and not others and then we see that they're marked at an angle, and figure they're also doing erosion control, although we don't entirely understand their system.

Gradually, we see the camp. It's unnervingly quiet, not a soul around, not a breeze, not a movement.

On our right are 15 or so scorched tents, ghostly gray. A supply truck has burned down to a skeleton of twisted metal squares and rectangles. Yet, less than a few yards away, a group of picnic tables remains untouched. Across the road, the meadow shines so green it feels electric by contrast, bordered by healthy aspens—perhaps a case of the aspens protecting part of the forest. One structure burned down to its metal roof and brick fireplace. Other buildings just look singed. Some look normal, at least from the outside.

The camp lost 80 percent of its trees and it will take at least a half-million dollars to rebuild and replace tents and other camping equipment, sheds, and bathrooms. They will have to rebuild their entire water system.

Russ and I take photos, Joe explores a bit, and Gwyn keeps walking. We meet again when we get to the Red Trail, which goes up Bear Creek and is one of our favorite hikes. We all want to see how it looks.

The road at the foot of the trail is flooded, which is a surprise—we had naively thought the recent rains were soaking into the dry earth, hydrophobic soil or not. Silently, we look for rocks to use as a path over the water and head up along the creek.

Russ and Gwyn lead the way and Joe stays behind with me as I poke along, puffing and panting in my own breathless way.

The trail itself retains most of its former beauty. The creek sounds like a meditation CD, slushing and gurgling over rocks. Its narrow path is bordered with wildflowers—purple flax, penstemon, and blue bells. The pines and spruce are shades of green, the grass thick and high.

We see no signs of fire damage until we turn around and look back at the camp and see the rocks where it started. The forest is black there, as are the rocks. I feel a bit like Lot's wife looking back at destruction, but this must be permissible because I do not become salt.

After about 45 minutes, I finally make it to where the rest are waiting for me. Together, we walk by Ed's favorite tree, the gigantic ponderosa pine. It is brilliantly alive and healthy. We pat it affectionately.

We're now at the farthest edge of our ridge and, once again, we can see for miles. The East Peak is now on our right, the meadow in front an emerald apron, with a series of ridges jutting up like a burnt orange, black, and green Lego village.

And, most important, it's mainly downhill from here. But that loses a bit of its charm as we slip and slide in a sludge of ash and mud. Our legs do scissor stretches as we carefully work our way down. One leg slides forward, one slips back. Surprisingly, no one falls, but we look like beginning ice skaters.

We see a bear print going up one hill and, next to it, about a three-foot long print where the bear slid, five claws making indentations like fat strips of chocolate licorice. Seems the bears have as much trouble here as we do.

We finally make it to the meadow where the ground is flat and dry, and we can walk normally. All along the way, we have seen downed trees angled deliberately across the hillsides. We hear saws when we get close to the water tank that had been next to an old chicken coop, part of a 1940's homestead. The coop has been burned to nothingness and the tank is on its side.

On the hillside, we see Dave and his brother Daryl working above the spring that fills the tank. They rest their saws on the ground and come over to talk with us. They teach us their process: Cut dead trees and place them at a 30-degree angle along the grade of the hill, then fill any gaps underneath with branches or what little foliage is left on the trees. This slows the water and reduces erosion.

We chat a little, but they are busy. Plus, we're exhausted and none of us has much small talk in us right now. We wish them luck, thank them for their help, and soon are on the cottage porch, drinking Diet Coke and breathing hard. Ed has been working nearby, hears us, comes and sits down with his tea. He, Joe, and Russ make a plan to begin sawing trees that afternoon. Gwyn and I will clean up the smaller branches and twigs.

We begin working on the steepest grades, especially on our paths, as they become streams when it rains. The men cut the trees and move them onto the paths. Gwyn and I fill underneath with brush. We borrow Jim Bryant's industrial chipper, which was saved from the fire in their concrete block garage, and chip the trees we don't use for erosion, in an assembly line. Ed and Joe and Russ cut the trees, Gwyn and I pull out the small branches and make a pile of them. Then Ed comes with the chipper and we all load the wood in. The chipper can take wood four inches in diameter and chew it up into 1- to 3-inch chips. We wear goggles and face masks because sawdust and tiny rockets of wood can fly back from the machine. And the chipper's high-pitched squeal echoes for miles, so we also wear earplugs.

This continues through the summer. Often, it's just Ed and Joe up there cutting, while Gwyn works in her garden and on smaller paths with her own small chainsaw, and I retreat to the cabin to work on the health writing I've done since retiring from teaching. We don't really take a serious count of the trees we've cut; Joe stops counting at 75 around the cabin alone. In a forest with thousands of dead trees, it's small progress.

It's also messy progress, as the ash clings to everything: face, ears, hats, gloves, shoes, glasses. One day, Joe comes home after a morning of cutting. He's chuckling.

"You should see Ed—all you can see are his eyes. The rest of him is ash."

I laugh and Joe scowls at me, not getting the joke: He does not have a mirror, so he does not know that all I can see of him are his eyes. The rest of him is ash.

We set up outdoor sinks to wash off before we go inside. We take off our work clothes and leave them on the deck.

Russ comes up again for a weekend and brings his brother Dan. They work nonstop cutting and placing trees in the path of potential flooding, chipping the leftovers. Their younger bodies are a blessing and they leave the forest in much better shape. Just watching them is exhausting, and we are grateful they shared their sweat and energy with us.

We begin talking about getting a logger to help—the trees are still green inside and could make decent lumber. Because I become less and less useful with tree cutting—the ash triggers my emphysema and I cough like Mimi in *La Boheme*—my job becomes trying to find outside helpers. I fail. I call a company in Trinidad, but it is out of business. I find one in southern New Mexico, but the owner says our land is too far a drive. Harlan and Frank begin talking with a logger working out of Pueblo and I put in numerous calls to him with no callback. I understand that working with black trees is messy, but it seems like a good opportunity.

Still, Colorado is full of burned trees. Ours are nothing special.

10. I Revere This Place

Hope looks a lot like weeds. Scrub oaks and locusts are the first trees to grow back, little pokes of green popping out of the grey, wounded earth. We call them weed trees—they pop up everywhere, crowding out larger, more permanent growth. But they are green, and we initially welcome them for erosion control.

Locusts provide nitrogen to our sick soil, but they grow so thick and fast that they can crowd out anything else in their path. They're also packed with thorns, so navigating through them is painful. The only way to totally kill them is to cut them and treat the stump to keep it from growing. Sounds workable in a typical yard, we're dealing with hundreds of acres, so this would be a full-time job, and how do we prioritize that over the cutting and erosion control?

Leaving the trees alone makes as much ecological sense as cutting them—perhaps more so because it uses fewer machines and the gas that powers them. Some will eventually fall on their own, providing nutrients for the soil. Others, if the roots hold, will stand for years, until they're whittled with wind, birds, insects, and time. Foresters warn us not to walk in the forest in a big wind as trees could fall on us. We heed their advice.

Musk thistles grow wildly, with great delight, and would consume us all if we didn't keep an eye on them. They have showy purple flowers on maliciously spiked, prickly stems. And with few other plants to stop them, they shoot up to human height within weeks of first showing their nasty little sprouts. We pull them easily because the ground is so brittle, and we dump large piles of them in the road, where they wither and die. The trick is to get them before they blossom and spread their evil seeds. Canada thistle, a smaller and even more insidious cousin, fills what little space is left. They grow and develop seeds and spread wildly before we even notice them.

We also have a bumper crop of sage-green mullein, its beguiling, velvety leaves masking the fact that, like thistle, it is an invasive species and seems to want to grow wherever and however it damn well pleases. Apparently ancient Romans used the yellow stalks, which can easily and quickly grow to 8-foot lengths, for hair rinse and also extracted the color for dye.

Both thistle and mullein have medicinal uses. Chewing thistle leaves can reduce toothache pain, rubbing it on your ear can calm an earache, and the flower can ease digestive problems—once you get rid of the prickles. If we work with thistles too long, without leather gloves, the tips of our fingers begin to get numb.

Mullein can help with respiratory problems, soothing irritated membranes and making coughs more productive. Given that we all have one or more of these health problems, we perhaps should be harvesting our plants. We've talked about it, but the logistics—how to harvest, cull, manufacture, distribute, and all that—overwhelmed us and we decided that was just another thing we don't need to do.

In late summer, we discover tiny aspen shoots and we welcome them like the birth of a cherished child. We mark their little groves with surveyor's tape, so we don't drive over these beautiful little fire fighters with the chipper or trucks or clumsily stomp on them with our boots. They are sure signs of the beginning of a new forest and are some of the most beautiful trees in the forest. Aspen groves have one giant underground root, so as long as that root was not burned, they will regrow. And soon we see them all over the ridge. They like sunlight and, with all the shade trees burned, they have plenty of it.

It will take years before we see any new evergreens and we may have to plant some of those ourselves. But for now, we have aspens.

We buy several 55-pound bags of mountain grass seed, a mixture of brome, rye, and wheatgrass, and scatter it over the ridge. I focus on the top of the cemetery trail, which has burned down to bare ground. We buy a wheeled grass spreader but it's too hard to navigate on our uneven, rocky ground, so we do much of it by hand. The grass grows beautifully, with much remaining at the top of the hill, and some washing down into the gully. That's OK. We need erosion help everywhere.

I envision turning the ridge into one large, beautiful meadow, with a few aspens scattered about and, eventually, pines and firs. Essentially creating my own groomed meadow up there. That's a bit ambitious, given I am throwing seeds and using a hand rake. I go back to pulling thistles and planting grass, making progress, however small.

We hear of neighbors bringing in giant excavator mulchers that chew up entire trees and leave chips behind. We decide to stick with being hands-on, unless we can find a logger to help, a quest that has remained as elusive as my meadow.

The piles of chips grow like acne all over our land. Some by the creek, where Joe and Ed have cut willows; some by the road where they've trimmed aspens, locusts, and pines; and heartbreaking mounds on the ridge, made of fir, pine, aspens, locusts. Mini mountains rising three, four, five feet tall. They still smell fresh because the sap flows when we cut the trees, the life still oozing from burned hulls.

Gwyn and Ed use some chips for the garden and for landscaping. We rake some onto our path to the road and around the cabin. Joe spends a day working on our meditation garden, a grandiose name for our 12-foot square plot on the other side of the creek, trimmed with rocks and irises we got from our neighbor Pat several years ago, with a makeshift bench in the middle—a chunk of weathered railroad tie on top of concrete blocks. The wood had been our front step when we first built the cabin; the blocks are left over from the pilings on which the cabin sits.

Several years ago, Joe made a plank that angles down to the creek—an 8-foot stretch of lumber studded with wood strips for footholds. The plank connects to a little footbridge that sits about two feet above the creek and leads to the meditation garden. He always intended to make proper steps by digging railroad ties into the bank, but there's just too much to do up here in even a good year, so most of our ideas live only in our heads.

The bridge is a favorite of our four smallest visitors, our grandsons Tarin and Eli and Ed and Gwyn's grandsons Connor and Caden. Tarin and Eli have been known to fish for tuna from it, with surprisingly little luck. Connor and Caden use it to launch boats.

When Joe is finished primping the garden, I walk carefully down the plank and over the bridge and sit for a moment on the bench. Ellen staked out this site several years ago, wanting easier, less weedy access to the creek. It eventually morphed into the meditation garden—I had envisioned sitting there and doing yoga, but too many bugs decided to keep me company, so now I just sit there for a few minutes, take deep breaths, and give thanks for this beauty.

After the fire a friend said, "Maybe this will make you appreciate your cabin more."

"How could I possibly appreciate it more?" I asked. I revere this place.

11. Sleeping with an Ear to the Creek

The mountain disappears behind an ominous sky. It is raining hard up there and has been for an hour or so. We've had about three inches at the cabin, unheard of before the fire.

I stand at the door, watching the creek rise. It has always been a mild thing, about two feet wide and a foot deep, a calm, meandering stream; in recent years, it has usually disappeared altogether by July or August. Tonight, it is moving swiftly under Joe's little wooden bridge, but it remains safely away from the cabin.

I look out at Mr. Green Jeans, ironically parked for the first time ever on the culvert over the creek. I had washed it that day and neither of us got around to moving it back onto the road behind the cabin, where it is always parked. Always. We both thought of doing it, but then asked, "Why?" What harm could there be in leaving it by the creek? We plan to go to church the next day, so we'll just move it then.

I shut the door and go inside.

We have started watching a movie on my computer. We have no television, so we use our Netflix CDs on my MacBook. We sit together on the couch with the computer on the old wooden icebox we use as coffee table, me cuddled into Joe and covered with an afghan our neighbor Pat made for us a few years ago.

The rain builds and beats down on our metal roof, which makes it sound even louder. Worried, I get up and check the creek again. Still in its banks, still OK. The meditation garden has a few rivulets of water rushing over it, but Joe's handiwork remains largely intact.

I shut the door and again head to the couch. I take about four steps, then I hear a crashing roar from outside. I run back to the door.

"Holy smokes!" I cry, and Joe runs up behind me to see. The creek has swollen to 30 feet wide and probably six feet deep, a good ten times its size. It is roiling and thundering past, pushing tree trunks in its wake. Thankfully, it has spread to the meadow side, not toward the cabin. It's still in its banks here.

It is a flash flood and I barely missed the wall of water storming down.

We look across the creek at our well, which we have powered by a generator that we keep in the meadow. We had stored it, a fancy Honda model, in a shed by the cabin, but the gas fumes bothered me, so Joe moved it next to the well and covered it with a garden cart.

We watch silently as the water picks up the generator and moves it as though it were a rubber duck. It weighs 120 pounds. It finally gets caught in a willow and stays there, wobbling and waterlogged.

Mr. Green Jeans looks safe so far, above the flood on the culvert. The water comes about three inches up to his tires, but he stays put.

We watch, awed. The creek's idea of flooding has usually been to rise about a foot. Not this. Never this.

The upstream vegetation is largely burned away, so nothing slows the water down; it just gains momentum as it rushes by.

We put on rain suits and go onto the deck and watch, keeping an eye on the generator and the SUV, watching logs whiz by like toothpicks.

I wonder if Ed and Gwyn know about this. Their house is about 50 feet from the creek, all uphill, but Gwyn's amazing garden would be right in the flood's path. I call and Ed answers. I tell him we have a flood. They, too, had been watching a movie and had thought they heard a roar, but were far enough away to not be seriously concerned.

He goes out to check their damage and, within half an hour, walks down to our place, wearing his raincoat and hip boots. We see his high-powered flashlight before we see him.

"Who could have imagined?" he says.

"Not us," I say unnecessarily and ask about the garden.

"It's fine," he says. "The wall stopped the water —the flood went around, on both sides." The wall is one source of Gwyn's bad back—it's 4-feet tall and 12-feet long, made of stones she collected from the hillsides. We helped a little, giving her a birthday present of 13 rocks one year, painting a letter on each one to spell *Happy Birthday*. But, like idiots, we let her put them into the wall herself; the better present would have been to actually help with the wall.

Still, the wall saved the garden.

"But our stock tank is gone," Ed says. He figures it contained about 100 gallons of water, making it weigh a bit more than 800 pounds. The flood just picked it up and pushed it downstream somewhere.

The meditation garden is under water and our bridge has washed away. Later, Joe finds it in pieces in the trees downstream. It takes Ed days to finally find his stock tank—it is covered by mud about 50 feet from where it had been.

The generator does not fare so well. Joe spends a couple of days cleaning the mud out of its various parts and pieces. Ed helps clean the carburetor. Still, it starts then stalls and sputters. Joe takes it to town, and they clean it out more. It lasts the rest of the summer, but it is clear we will need to replace it.

Mr. Green Jeans is fine. The next morning, Joe goes out in his mud boots and drives the SUV off the culvert and up to the road. It is a slow, mucky ride in the mud, ash and slime, so the wheels whirl and spin. Joe puts it in low gear 4-wheel drive and makes it out, shimmying up the hill, and the truck has been fine ever since, bless its teenage heart.

The stench of the flood remains for weeks. A murky, sour, mildewed smell of dank water and mud and organic detritus. I think of the survivors of recent hurricanes—Maria, Harvey, Irma, Katrina, Irene, Sandy—and how those people had to dig their entire lives out of the mud, inhaling this toxic air. My eyes fill and I cry silently for them, for me, and for the world we share.

In the next few days, we clean trees and bushes out of the culvert and try to clear the biggest trunks and branches out of the meadow. Ed usually mows the field every fall and uses the hay to feed their horses for the rest of the year. The grass had just started growing well enough to be a decent crop this year and now it is matted down with mud and broken trees. Ed ultimately gets some hay, but not enough for an entire year.

The rains and resulting floods continue off and on for the rest of the summer. The meditation garden is a muddy glob. The bridge washes out with each flood and Joe finally decides not to replace it. The railroad tie ends up in the willows; the cement blocks are scattered in the sludge, landing this way and that.

Dave tells us that the scout camp has had several destructive floods, with boulders rolling down Bear Creek. The old log cabins where Dave's grandmother and uncles once lived are ruined by floodwaters. The camp is closed for the rest of the year.

Now, when it rains at night, I sleep with one ear attuned to sounds of the creek. I imagine a wall of water descending onto the cabin and gushing in through the windows above my desk, closest to the creek, of the cabin ending up on its edge like the homes we saw in Vermont after Hurricane Irene.

• • •

Josh visits, and we hike up to the ridge and over by Doc's house; he wants to see what the fire has done. We go part of the way with him, but he is younger and stronger and soon he takes the high road and we take the low one. We walk over the dike and look across to see Josh's long, lean form moving along the far ridge. The sight lines are so much better without all those trees. Damn the sight lines.

We meet him on our way back.

"How was it?" I ask.

"Not as bad as I expected," he says. "There are still a lot of pockets of green."

That's encouraging, I guess. As with all things in life, your perspective governs your feelings. But then your feelings tint your perspective. He's looking at a forest half alive. I see a forest half dead.

"But you know the cliff you want us to push you off?" he asks. I nod. "The trees are all gone now, so there's nothing to break your fall." OK, a word of explanation: I have a mild fear of getting some form of dementia and being a burden on my family while I live without a life. Ed says when he is ready to die, he is going to go off into the woods to sit under a tree without food or water until his body totally gives out. Then vultures and other animals will eat what's left; he'll be giving himself back to nature. I don't believe him, and I don't think he does either.

Still, when I first saw the cliff a decade or so ago, with a drop off of about 100 feet, I figured that would be a more elegant way to go. Just get somebody to push me off, if I get to the point where I don't know enough to jump on my own. I told that to Josh and Ellen on one of our hikes. Ever the detail man, Josh walked up to the edge and looked over.

"Too many trees," he said. "You'd get stuck going down."

We all laughed amiably at my macabre fantasy.

But now, the fire has cleared my path.

"Good to know," I say.

We walk back silently, all lost in our thoughts of death, destruction, dinner.

Josh's bike survived the fire safely in our shed. It needs some brake work and a new tire, but it is soon ready for his rides around the mountain paths and along the side roads. The week before he came, we scouted routes and found that roads west, toward La Veta, were still green and untouched, with the beauty we had once considered normal; the fire did not race that direction. Clearly, westerly winds sent the burn from the camp to us and further east. If the wind had only been from the other direction, I think. I am wishing ill of my neighbors to the west. Yes, I am. My first wish, though, would be no fire at all.

But still, there are the *what if*s. What if helicopters had doused the fire at its origin, when it was just smoldering? What if we had bought land there instead of here? What if there had been no wind at all? What if the trees and grasses had not been so dry? What if we could have culled our forest better? What if it weren't getting hotter and hotter here? What, what, what?

We recommend a route to Josh: a wonderful ride through a county road with the East Peak on the left and the West Peak in front, the Sangre de Christo range on the right. And cows along the path, but whatever. Josh is not afraid of cows. And no sign of burns unless you look closely up the side of the East Peak. Pastoral and unblemished.

It's a 42-mile ride, going to La Veta then to Walsenburg, where we meet him at Corine's Mexican Restaurant. He has his usual chicken fried steak smothered in green chili and I watch in awe, thinking of how many calories he has burned and how many he can enjoy guilt-free. I savor my one enchilada with green chili, delighting in my food and in my son and in my son's delight in his food, his ride, his mountain.

The weather is a godsend during his visit—warm enough, but not hot, with a couple of decent rains. The creek rises several feet during one storm, but luckily my constant watch keeps it from going over its banks.

Things get a bit more ominous on our way to drop Josh off at the airport in Colorado Springs: We drive through a wicked sandstorm, unable to even see the car ahead of us at some points. The wind comes in short gales, with an occasional clear stretch allowing us to get our bearings, then another gust of sand dashing into the windshield. The dry ground and increasingly windy days have made such storms far more common and have caused several crashes on the highways near Pueblo.

We finally get to the airport, hug Josh goodbye, and head back into another sandstorm. The sky toward the mountain is especially black, and I check the weather on my phone. There's a serious storm south of Pueblo, which we will have to drive through.

I've had enough of fighting with the weather, so we stop at a motel on the north side of Pueblo. Phyllis is out of town, otherwise we would impose ourselves on her. The motel gives us toothpaste and brushes and we go to the Goodwill across the highway for a change of clothes: a new jacket and slacks for me, and a shirt and pants for Joe, which we wash in the motel laundry. Decked out in our fresh and fancy fashions, we go to a restaurant in an old Protestant church, close to Pueblo Catholic High, where I went to school. I remember walking by this place and wondering how it looked inside, what those Protestant-kind-of-folks did in church. It makes a nice restaurant, and we have a martini and broiled fish.

As usual, I enjoy our visits to civilization, but I am ready to head back. We have breakfast at a coffee shop on Union Street, then aim Mr. Green Jeans at the Interstate and the East Peak. An hour and a half later we get to the cabin and are met with gorgeous blue skies and a gleaming mountain, as though the storms were just an illusion. But we know the clouds can open again, so we get ready.

The Colorado State Forest Service provides sandbags for flood protection. Joe and Ed go to the scout camp and get a pickup load and place them at our problem spots—by the garden, at the bottom of our trails up to the ridge, along Dominic's road across the meadow. We think about adding some between the creek and the cabin, but it really doesn't make sense, as our danger would be in the first minutes of a flash flood and sandbags wouldn't help.

Gwyn's garden remains safe, as does the cabin. We notice the beginning of gouges on the face of the mountain where water has washed out rocks and soil. The mountain is physically changing, scars are building and expanding on its face, with chunks shifting from higher to lower ground, and ruined trees standing watch, their branches cracking in the wind, falling in the rain, as the mountain soil washes down to our valley.

I have often wondered, after the fire, if I am grieving what I personally lost up here, or if I am grieving for the land itself, for what it and its bears and eagles and elk have lost. These mountains have nearly 60 years of memories for me, starting with our family visits when I was in grade school, then to college geology field trips to study the dikes and climb the West Peak with my best friends at the time, to the family time we have spent here living and watching nature flaunt her beauty at our doorstep. So, yes, it is personal.

But I believe the land is sacred and that it is a blessing to everything that enters it, every plant, person, and animal. And that it needs and deserves our protection and respect. It doesn't have to actually do anything for us; just being is its gift.

Ed, Gwyn, Joe and I have built small up here, not the McMansions we see elsewhere in the mountains; those make me cringe. We try to limit our use of resources by going solar and using composting toilets. Our refrigerators and stoves are LP gas, and the refrigerator is tiny—only 8 cubic feet total, including a miniscule freezer. We heat with wood from downed trees. Our road is dirt. Ed and Gwyn have a wringer washer and an outdoor clothesline. Joe and I are more wasteful; we go to the Laundromat in Trinidad and, while we're there, feast on Mexican food that is as good as it gets anywhere.

In general, though, we have replaced our urban creature comforts with the comfort and solace of the land. We try to not take more than we give, to make our living here reciprocal.

But the longer we live with the results of the fire, the more difficult that becomes, the more overwhelmed we are with what the land needs and our own inadequacy to provide that.

Our responses reflect our personalities.

Ed: The land will regrow, so we need to just help it a little, by doing erosion control and cutting trees that are in danger of falling.

Gwyn: We need to plant grass in the bare areas and replant the trees and cut all the new weeds.

Joe: Forests know how to rebuild; we have to make sure we are careful not to hurt ourselves trying to do too much.

Me: Let's focus on grass for now and see what happens next year.

Of course, we all reserve the right to change our minds multiple times in a day.

As we hike during one of our visits with Russ, he talks about the belief that this land is hallowed ground. And, he says, that means the fire also was sacred, a cleaning and a rebirth.

A priest friend reminds me that this is a resurrection. A time of building new beauty, even a time of consecration.

On good days, I get that. Yes, to the rebirth and the rebuilding and to nature's plans. To a resurrection. On bad days, though, it is just a damn fire that burned down our beautiful forest.

12. Communal Grief

At the end of the summer, Dave invites us to a barn dance organized by neighbors to celebrate surviving the fire. It is in a rancher's equipment building, a 40x80-foot pole barn with 14-foot ceilings and truck-sized garage doors that are open to let in the mountain air. I marvel at it and the owner tells me I could have one like it for a little over $100,000. I think about raiding my retirement fund and then realize I actually have no earthly need for a giant pole barn.

During the party, we thank the neighbors who helped fight the fire and I have a chance to meet some of the people who helped save our cabin. We applaud them, most of us with tears streaming down our cheeks. Some neighbors tell their stories. A man whose house close to the scout camp survived told of what he saw in his motion-activated camera—firefighters with axes running by, others with hoses, the fire coming close, then receding, animals running in fear.

Then somebody puts music on, and we dance, at which time I regret trying to fit in by wearing my cowboy boots. But it is heartening to feel like one of these people, many of whom have known one another all their lives, as their families have ranched these plains for generations.

We leave earlier than most partiers, the soft thumping of the music and the light from the barn fading into the night as we drive off into the absolute darkness of a mountain road.

But the end of summer is also the end of our time up here.

My high school reunion is in early September, so we plan to pack up, winterize the cabin, head to Pueblo to see my aged classmates, then drive home to Iowa.

Leaving is a mixed bag of emotions for us. We look forward to our dishwasher, washing machine and dryer, television, and flush toilets in Des Moines. But the price for that is leaving this serenity and beauty.

Joe seldom reminds me of my dad—he is much, much mellower—except for what comes out of his mouth when he is working on a challenging project. Then he goes into drunken sailor mode.

Our water system was a challenge when Ed first put it in and has remained one through the years, as Joe and Ed bit by bit have replaced PVC pipe with copper and old assorted connectors with new assorted connectors in a mass of loops and turnoffs and joints, all of which can, and often do, leak.

Because our pipes could freeze, we need to drain the system then fill it with antifreeze and shut it off. We have instructions that Ed wrote 20 years ago, and we have been following them for 20 years, but usually something goes wrong, some *on* switch ends up off, the hot water valve accidentally flows into the cold water, or Joe forgets where he was and has to retrace his steps, usually messing one up. I pack up the cabin and leave the water system to Joe and his potty mouth.

Packing overall is a pain—everything off the deck and into the shed, except for the rugs and boot box, which go into the cabin once we're out. And all the food that will not make it over the winter either gets pitched or boxed or put into our camping cooler to take with us. No matter how we plan, we usually end up with a random selection of leftovers in the fridge: six green olives, a cup of salad dressing, five teaspoons of mayo, and two eggs. We have no garbage disposal and we can't put food in the dumpster that we share with Harlan and Pat because it would smell up the whole thing and attract bears. We have a compost pile about a quarter mile from the cabin—far enough for bears to root in it and leave us alone—and we drop the leftover food there before we leave. Bigger items we dump in Ed and Gwyn's manure pile.

We leave the land a bit healthier than when we arrived after the fire in July, with a fuzz of green—probably locust trees—poking up along the blackened hillsides. Still, the meadow is as lush as it's ever been.

First, we stop and visit with Harlan and Pat. They show us the projects they are planning in the hopes of making their home more fire resistant: more concrete trim around their house, fewer trees close by. As we leave, we are again stunned by the charred hill opposite their home. When they sit outside, they now look the other direction, at the batch of unburned trees in their backyard.

Our visit with Pearl and Fiore is bittersweet. Pearl is in shock and not processing things well, so there is a lot of repetition. But she hugs us hard and welcomes us with tears in her eyes. Fiore tells us the stories we have already heard—about the giant rattler his cousin Dominic found on our land one year, the bear he wasn't supposed to shoot but did and then had to bury. We don't mind. He tells a good story. Plus, we fear we will not see him again, so this is precious time. We hope that the energy he is showing might mean his diagnosis is not as serious as we think.

As we drive away, we look up the hill at the cross that marks a small cemetery, where Dominic, his mother, and other family members are buried. I remember meeting Dominic's mom, who had to be in her late 80s, the first time I came up here. She kept talking about her husband and we asked where he was. "He's up under the apple tree," she said. It took us a few months to realize that he was in one of the graves.

· · ·

Forest fires and their aftereffects are a hot topic at my reunion. Several classmates live near Colorado Springs, which has had two huge fires in two years: Waldo Canyon last year and Black Forest this year, just a week before ours. Together they burned nearly 33,000 acres.

One classmate lives in Manitou Springs, which is below Waldo Canyon, and which has borne the brunt of flooding. It's a scenic, historic town that has been almost shut down all summer. She has a small stream behind her house and, like me, on rainy nights she sleeps with one ear focused on the sounds of rushing water; she's always prepared to escape.

Another classmate lives in Black Forest and lost his house. His insurance paid for the structure, but he has to rebuild it where it is, and he will have to live in a burn zone.

The Black Forest was Colorado's most expensive fire, destroying more than 500 homes. A couple in their 50s was killed, caught in their garage before they could escape.

The entire Colorado Springs area is highly populated, with large, expensive homes in the mountains. By contrast, our area has a home or two every few miles, and most of those are small, many of them built by the owners. The economic impact of the Colorado Springs fires dwarfs ours. But we had unspoiled wilderness that was priceless.

The day after the reunion we start our drive back to Iowa. The clouds along the Front Range are menacing as we leave Pueblo and get meaner and meaner as we drive north. As we get onto Highway 24 in Colorado Springs, the rain starts and by the time we are on the bridge over Fountain Creek it is a full-out deluge. I get a warning on my phone to avoid Fountain Creek. Water is flowing across the road; it's already several inches deep in intersections. Teeth clenched, we stay the course and finally climb out of the valley and head to the east, toward Limon. The rain lessens the farther we get from the mountains. Soon it becomes a trickle. We breathe.

Usually, we look behind us and say goodbye to the mountains. Today, we see behind us only somber hues of grey. We look ahead quietly, grimly.

What an almost unbearably awful summer.

The weather on the entire ride home is nasty—rain, fog, chilly temps for mid-September. In my paranoia, I feel like we have a cloud over our heads. And all the way through eastern Colorado, Nebraska, and western Iowa, we do.

What are we to make of the summer we just left behind? Right now, nothing. We are exhausted, our minds and bodies spent. We follow the familiar path home. We do not think too philosophically; we have no profound discussions. There is no doubt in our minds that the landscape has changed, especially for us in the mountain and for a good portion of the American West. The frontier my grandparents first saw in the early 1900s is now a mass of construction and stress. Even the high desert where I went horseback riding in college and never saw a soul, feeling like I was just discovering the state, even that is now full of housing developments with streets named after what they replace: Redhawk and Bobcat and Peregrine. There is even a Bridle Trail that starts where I used to ride on an actual bridle trail of cacti and yucca plants. Now it's lined with homes. Condos cover the mountains, especially in ski resorts.

And all that battered earth is now being pummeled by driving rain that has no welcoming ground or vegetation to soak into, so it heads downhill, often with the overdeveloped countryside in its way.

But for now, we just follow the road and don't think too much.

PART TWO

The Stressed Earth and Its Creatures

13. I Didn't Expect Fear

Once again, I am doing what I do up here every chance I get: looking out the window at the mountain, soaking it up, breathing in its strength and calm and beauty. It's June 7, 2014, late in the afternoon on our first day back for this summer, almost a year after the fire.

I peer out, expecting calm. Then gasp. Flaming red and orange clouds radiate from the horizon up toward the peak.

I am not sure of what I see—something gorgeous or something terrifying.

"Hon!" I call. "Look at this!"

Joe looks out the window and then both of us head to the deck to see more clearly.

An amazing sunset? Another fire?

"What is it?" I ask.

We watch and wait, looking for the movement that would indicate this is smoke rather than clouds.

The colors remain static, unshifting. There's no smell. Can we trust that, as is almost always the case—except for that one time—it's the sun, burning 93 million miles away and sending a gorgeous reflection to Earth? We can trust that, yes. It's a halting trust, a trust that requires effort and some internal dialogue:

It's just the sunset, it's just the sunset, it's just the sunset. Really? Is it just the sunset? Really, it is. It's just the sunset.

We inhale in appreciation of the beauty and the lack of new chaos.

This fearfulness is new. Once a sunset was just a sunset, a raincloud a blessed sign of needed moisture. This year, though, I am on my guard. Our refuge, our place of peace has an overlay of danger. My confidence in the steadfastness of the mountain and its valleys and ridges has been shaken.

I didn't expect fear. I thought this was the year all would return to natural. Last year was the big event, the disaster. This year is our resurrection. It does not turn out that way. The year after the fire is even harder, with floods, landslides, and confused wildlife. I had a sense of chutzpah right after the fire, an assuredness that we could ride this out just fine. And we will indeed ride it out. And we may be fine eventually, but the timeline is far longer and more jagged and uncertain than I thought.

We returned full of enthusiasm, naiveté, and bluster. We are going to help rebuild this forest, yes we are. Joe and I ordered 60 evergreen seedlings from the National Forest Service; Ed and Gwyn got 200. We'll plant them on our back ridge. We expect a third to a half to make it, but we feel empowered by our plan.

It's a start. We have at least part of it figured out.

Our loss continued over the winter when Fiore died in December. We know that Pearl is not doing well—stress, early signs of dementia, I'm not sure—and Melva and her family are now living with her, so we don't stop and visit this time. We'll call and make an appointment for later. As we drive by, we see a new deck on the house and a kennel with several German Shepherds. A young man is riding a horse by the pond. We wave and he waves back, but none of us have the slightest idea who the others are. Ours is the rural wave: one hand casually extended above the steering wheel, barely visible, but clearly noted if you don't do it.

Harlan and Pat are not home, so no visit there either. But we see the effects of the logger they have working their land—the hillside past their house has been thinned and looks nicely groomed. Farther down the valley, we see enormous piles of uprooted trees dumped on the side of the road—mounds of firs and pines as tall as a house, most burned, but some still green with healthy needles. Harlan had to enlarge his road up the ridge for the logger's trucks, which meant some good trees had to go as well.

We have decided against full-scale logging and plan to just team up with Mom Nature and do what we can, cutting the biggest and most unstable trees that could fall and be dangerous, and continuing our endless chipping.

The hillsides remain fields of ebony poles with green underbrush—locust trees, scrub oak, and a few precious aspens. Lots of weeds, too—thistle especially. But the grass is lush, a brilliant green. More evergreens have died over the winter, and our few patches of green forest have blotches of rust, with trees more than a century old breathing their last bits of mountain air, delayed effects of the fire.

It's still heartbreaking to drive by empty ground where the Bryants' home had been. An old cast iron heating stove sits where our junk shed had once stood—it survived the fire and was too heavy to move someplace else, although Ed was going to try. I told him to leave it there and I would plant geraniums around it. Maybe this year I will actually do that.

We drive by the 1940's Case tractor at the edge of our property. I was going to plant geraniums around it too. Maybe I will do that this year.

Mr. Green Jeans is jammed with the clothes and bedding we took home to wash last fall; food from our Iowa refrigerator and pantry plus some fresh things from Safeway in Walsenburg; Joe's chain saw and toolbox; my computer and random papers; our juicer; and who knows what else. The cabin is fully stocked with mountain clothes, dishes, spices, household items, and non-perishables.

As usual, my sweet brother has hooked up our water and turned on our propane for us, so the cabin utilities are on. And he's opened a couple of windows to air it out. I open more to let the mountain air in and prop the front door open so we can unload.

Joe hooks up the invertor that connects us to our solar panels and we now have power. I reach under the bed for the vacuum broom—we don't have any other place to store it, so it lives comfortably under the four-poster. I dig through unopened boxes and finally find the hand vac—we take it with us so we can keep it charged. Both are low-wattage appliances that pull little current and don't overload our minimal solar.

I begin vacuuming dead flies from the windowsills, around the woodstove, on the kitchen counter, in the bathtub, under the sink, inside the cabinets, under the couch and the bed, and even in the desk drawers. Then I wipe a layer of dust off the surfaces, scrub the sinks and bathtub, and we're ready to move in.

Joe goes down to the shed and gets our outdoor furniture and carries it up to the deck. I empty box after box and Joe takes them to the shed. After about five hours, things are more or less tidy and in place. The bed remains un-made but I feel too grimy to touch clean bedding, so we both shower and get ready to go to Ed and Gwyn's for dinner.

Tonight's dinner includes a large salad, with lettuce, tomatoes, and baby radishes from Gwyn's garden, spinach quiche, and wine. We talk about our plans for the year, primarily sowing our seedlings. Ed and Gwyn have already planted about 100. They have a system, moving in a circle that allows for easy watering with one of their ATVs. We keep thinking about getting an ATV. Maybe this year. For now, it's Mr. Green Jeans and our feet.

Before we plant, though, we have to get our little homestead readied—the path trimmed and covered with chips, flowers planted around the giant rock in front of the cabin, the bridge replaced after last year's floods.

Joe then puts out our hummingbird feeders—one on each side of the cabin, at roof level, about eight feet above the deck. He uses Pearl's recipe for the syrup, about ¼ cup sugar and a cup of water. It takes no time for the little birds to arrive, drink, and then begin their stunts—flying straight into the air and diving back down, almost to the ground. They are a contentious lot, fighting one another for one of the eight spouts. We have as many as 12 birds at a time, mostly broad-tailed and ruby-throated beauties. The rust-colored rufous usually show up in July, but they're already here. They are especially bossy, pushing other birds around just because they can, I guess. The birds have nests in a nearby scrub oak and in the willows by the creek, where they head at night. They show back up at sunrise and their cheeky chatter often wakes us up in the morning.

After four days at the cabin, we're ready to plant the trees. First, we have to figure which part of the land is Joe's and mine. We have no fences separating our property from the Bryants' or Ed and Gwyn's, but we have several reference points by the cabin. I start there and try to walk a boundary line, which I mark with orange surveyor's tape. I think I am pretty close and if we accidentally plant trees on somebody else's land, I am reasonably sure they will not mind.

The mountain had some decent snowpack over the winter and that, on top of a wet summer and spring, has left the ground moist and healthy. The grass is already a foot tall. Last year at this time it was so dry we couldn't walk five feet without our shoes getting covered in black dust. We're hoping that's a good sign. The areas we planted with grass seed last year are now thick and rich, and we feel like successful mountain botanists. Such cheek.

We help Ed and Gwyn plant one batch of trees to learn their process: dig about a 6-inch hole, plop in a fertilizer tablet, add a seedling, water it, replace the dirt, add the protective cage, and hold that in place with a dowel rod. Time and labor intensive, but time-tested and effective.

We ordered ponderosa pine and Douglas fir, two trees the Forest Service said were the most fire resistant. But then, last year at this time we had a forest full of ponderosa pine and Douglas fir and they are all now dead, so apparently the issue is broader and deeper than species type alone.

The space between trees is an important factor in wildfire management—a tree should have at least a 10-foot break between its branches and those of another tree so that a fire has less raw material to burn and spreads less easily from tree to tree. This means a slower fire, which is less destructive overall and easier to manage.

We plant our seedlings 10 to 12 feet apart, knowing some of our trees will die, so we should be allowing ample open space when they reach maturity and their crowns reach out to one another.

We plant in straight rows on both sides of an old logging road on the back ridge. When it's time to water, we'll bring Mr. Green Jeans up here with the water tank, then walk the rows. Should be good exercise.

We plant 20 that first day. I wear a 1980s striped Drake University sweatshirt for the occasion; I'd given it to Dad when I started teaching at Drake and inherited it when he died, so he is on the mountain with us in spirit. Dad never met a cussword he didn't like, but he also had an eye for beauty, so he is with us, cursing the goddamn son-of-a-bitch fire while appreciating the wildflowers blooming in the ashes.

Whole patches of ground are bright orange and yellow from wallflowers—apparently the ashes and extra moisture are a boon to these mountain beauties. They have more room to propagate now, and their colorful petals are even more striking in contrast to the black ground.

As we plant, we also yank thistles—small shoots at this point of the summer, and easy to pull from the damp ground.

It takes a week to plant all 60 trees, and it is generally rewarding work; we feel we are doulas aiding the mountain's rebirth. We have regular rain and it's a month before we feel the need to water. The trees remain alive and green. Some wild creature or other knocks over a few of the wire cages every now and then, but we easily right them.

Our watering system is a mix of elegant and enormously clumsy, with an eye to conservation of resources, primarily us. We load our 25-gallon water tank onto the back of Mr. Green Jeans and take our two watering cans and a roll of surveyor's tape. We fill each can from the tank; Joe takes one can and goes left and I take one and go right. We water closest to the road first, so the can gets lighter the farther we go. As we water, we add strips of orange tape to the dowel rod on each tree as our sign that we have watered that seedling. Then we move the car 15 feet or so and start on a new row. The next time we go, we take the tape off tree by tree to indicate which have been watered that day.

I imagine my dad watching us, suggesting a more efficient method. He was allergic to wasted steps—or wasted anything. But I tell him silently, *give me a break, I'm doing my best*, and then I realize he's not actually there and hasn't said a thing and I'm just talking to the wind

We're here to help Nature out. But we increasingly learn Nature has her own way and is more powerful than we are. And that's unnerving because we are a bunch of control freaks. It's a Prijatel trait, so Ed and I come by it genetically. Gwyn and Joe have developed it by marriage, as a defense mechanism. We are here in the first place because we're after our own piece of the wild but, while we are in awe of natural forces, we continue to try to impose our own order. Without order, what do we have?

We are frantic to regain our lost balance, but it's impossible to tell what's working, what we should do, why we should do it, and who we think we are. We're puny stick figures shaking our fists at elemental forces—fire, wind, water.

14. The Bear: A Premonition

I begin to have premonitions of a bear walking by our bed at night. I see him as he ambles past the dresser, his nose and ears coming first, then the lumbering body. Nothing ever happens in these visions; he's just walking by. We've had bears outside at night as long as we've been here, but they never tried to get in. Why, then, do I now imagine one inside?

Bears have awakened me at night several times over the years, a thud on the deck the sure sign of a heavyweight visitor. Twice I've looked out the window of our kitchen door and found a bear looking back. Both times, they sniffed, shrugged, and left. Most disturbing was the night I heard our garbage can crash over—it was filled with containers we thought we had cleaned thoroughly. An unearthly rip and crunch reverberated through the dark. The next morning, we found a Diet Coke can shredded in the grass. I apparently had not washed it as well as I had thought.

"Just imagine if that had been your head," Gwyn told me. I had not imagined that, but I certainly do now.

One year, we put our garbage sack in the junk shed and padlocked the door. The next morning, the lock remained intact on a slice of door that hung in tatters from a broken hinge. Our garbage was strewn all over the hillside.

We've adapted, and we no longer leave trash of any kind out, even cans, because the smell can linger, and bears have one of the best senses of smell of any animal on Earth—some say *the* best. It's seven times that of a bloodhound, or 100 times that of a human; they can smell food up to 20 miles away. Anything with sugar or fish is especially tempting—we've cleaned tuna cans with Clorox and they still have lured bears. We take our relationship with bears seriously, making noise when we hike—I sing a little, *"Hello, bears, I'm a big human,*

human, human, human" when I walk by myself—and keeping doors and windows shut if we're gone. Early on, Phyllis carried pepper spray, but she never needed it and it's probably stashed under her sink somewhere, rusted shut.

I have a surprising level of complacency. I use earplugs to sleep so the bears' night wanderings don't wake me up. I figure, they're out there, I'm in here, what's the worry? I stubbornly cling to past reality, insisting that things will always be the way they have been, despite massive evidence to the contrary.

I don't dwell on my premonitions nor even wonder why they have appeared at this point. Yet, I have had forebodings before that have turned out to have merit. When Phyllis called me in 1993 to tell me Mom had liver cancer, I knew as soon as the phone rang that it was bad news. In fact, I was so wary when I answered that Phyllis started out by asking what was wrong with *me.* When I was going through cancer treatment, I awoke one morning with the clear thought that I was going to be fine. It was such a strong sense that it wiped out my worry. And, nine years later, all is still fine.

When I was in grade school, I was slow getting dressed one morning and Mom told me she would take me to school to get me there on time. *No,* I thought, *if you do, we'll have a wreck.* I did not say it out loud, but mom took me and, sure enough, a car hit us as we were crossing Indiana Avenue.

But that's all superstition, right? So, every night, I put my earplugs in and snooze right through whatever the bears want to do outside.

We see random bears regularly, and even when we don't see their furry selves, we find fresh scat on our walks. Two small bears scamper around the meadow and we wonder if they are the babies we saw last year. No mama with them. Did she die over the winter? Or are they old enough to be on their own? Moms typically stay with their babies through the middle of their second year, so it seems these are on their own a bit early, perhaps because mama bear was killed in the fire.

Teenage bears out wandering the woods without mom for direction. What could go wrong?

15. Walking Through A Poem

We drive to Trinidad to celebrate our anniversary and to enjoy a break from day-in-day-out devastation. Within half an hour, we've left our land of scorched trees and are in high desert, with yucca plants and cacti and sandy plateaus. Another half hour and we are in town, which sometimes feels like a different universe—all these people, all these buildings, all this stuff.

We get there in early morning, while it is still cool and the town is just waking up, owners opening their shop doors, watering their plants, and sweeping their sidewalks. The air is fresh, expectant of a new day. It's hearteningly ordinary.

I go to a coffee shop to research articles I am writing, update our Netflix queue, add a post or two to my cancer blog, and check tips on re-propagating a forest. Joe goes to the Laundromat under the interstate and does about six loads of laundry. I treat myself to a latte and pastry. Joe enjoys a sausage biscuit at McDonald's. We're both content with our tasks and treats.

Afterward, we run errands: We check antique stores for a chest that can serve as an end table and shelving to solve the everlasting problem of storage in the cabin, go to the hardware store for a kit to fix the tears in our front screen door, get two weeks' worth of groceries at Safeway, and on and on and boring on.

I don't think of the fire. Much.

We end the day with an early dinner at Rino's, an Italian restaurant with singing wait staff. We go there on most anniversaries and we tell them it's a special day and they sweetly serenade us, which makes us both cry.

This year, though, we opt to eat anonymously, mentioning nothing about our big day. We've had enough with attention, enough emotion. We burrow into our table, the two of us a solitary unit. *Leave us alone*, our body language says. We both have martinis and toast one another and the 44 years since we first said, "I do" in a tiny rural church on the outskirts of Des Moines. My stomach has been off since we've been in Colorado this year and I avoid the rich lobster in cream sauce I love, opting instead for a salad. We end by sharing tiramisu, although I only have a few bites.

Stress usually shows up first in my digestion, but I don't spend any time thinking about why my stomach is so tender now. It just is. So much of this year is like that: It just *is*.

The sun is beginning to set as we head back to the mountain, and the Sangre de Christo range glows deep purple against a poppy-colored sky, its snowy peaks still crisp white. The ridges and valleys of the Spanish Peaks are etched like wrinkles on a loved and lovely old crone. Sunrays rip through sheets of clouds, reminding me of the holy cards I got as a kid at St. Francis Xavier elementary school in Pueblo, the glowing shafts of light symbolizing God. Looks about right to me.

We slow down for cows in the road and stop for a group of deer darting in front of us. It's a mellow drive after a full day, yet my shoulders remain hunched, my muscles taut.

The sunset obscures the burn scars on the mountain—the scorched bands of trees, usually charcoal, now sparkle in the golden light. But even though I can't see the blackness, I can feel it.

I have my own burn scars, emotional wounds I keep behind a protective shell of artificial lightness to defend against my own darkness. I've not yet said it our loud, nor even silently, for that matter: *I'm depressed*. If I acknowledge it, what then? Baseline treatment for depression is keeping active, remaining productive, and surrounding yourself with meaning. I'm doing that, so I'm taking care of the problem, right? I'm fine. Just fine.

The truth is, though, as we drive back to face the mountain, I haven't even yet recognized how much I am hurting. It's only in the therapeutic process of writing about it that I now can see inside my own troubled head.

. . .

Harlan calls a few days later. I'm at my computer and Joe is on the front deck, replacing the screen in the door. We've repaired it with duct tape for years, but we finally have the needed screen to fix it right. This is often the way it is on the mountain: getting to town for supplies is such an ordeal that we tend to just jerry-rig things. It truly is a duct tape and WD-40 kind of life.

"Happy anniversary," Harlan says with forced brightness.

It takes me a minute to catch on. Our anniversary was days ago. But then I get it. It's the anniversary of the fire. When you are in the wilderness, you often don't even know what day it is, so missing a special date is unsurprising. And this date we could miss forever.

We have a neighborly chat about what's growing and what's not, about how his logging is going, what cutting and planting we're doing. It's the way we talk now: What are you doing to repair the damage? Is it working? All with the subtext: Are we doing the right thing? If so, what is that?

Harlan just bought a new machine that can cut trees at their base then slice them into chunks, hoping he can control some tree removal himself. I tell him we have considered getting a brush cutter, but we've shopped, discussed, reviewed, and ended up at our default setting: doing nothing.

Harlan laughs, but then agrees that a brush cutter would have helped groom an existing forest but would be puny against the forces we now face. We hang up with nothing resolved, but it is always good to know Harlan is there.

By now Joe has finished the screen and is hanging the door back up.

"Nice work!" I say. I look toward the meadow and smile at the lack of duct tape. Why did we wait so many years for this simple but profound improvement?

Ed drives up on his four-wheeler, which he has named Alice. He has a second one he has named Alice Too. Also a small tractor named Charles. Make of that what you will.

Ross is running ahead, Bella following behind. Ed and his dogs are headed to the grove across the meadow where he is cutting and chipping burned trees, making room for new growth. The hill on that side is more likely to see new evergreens than the back ridge where we're planting because so many large trees remain to shed pinecones and their healthy seeds.

He usually stops to visit in the morning, if only for a minute. Today, he throws his long legs over the ATV, with grace and movement that hide the joint pain that remains even after hip surgery. He slowly ambles up to the cabin.

"Beautiful morning!" he says.

"It is." I say. The sun is out, it is comfortable warm, and the air is clear. That's beauty.

I mention the anniversary to him. He grumbles and shrugs. OK, then. We talk a bit about Harlan and Pat's logging and about what we're doing and we are once again in the same circular discussion. We all tire of it and Ed gets back onto Alice and putts across the meadow, finally out of sight in the brush.

• • •

I've been helping water Gwyn's garden this year, and we have reached a plan in which I do it on even days, they do it on odd days.

The garden is again a marvel. Gwyn starts 250 plants or more in the winter and babies them for months until she can tuck them into the earth. It's a plot the size of a single car garage that grows lettuce blends, spinach, broccoli, bok choy, onions, radishes, squash, corn. The small adjoining greenhouse has peppers and tomatoes. It's all organic, a healthy work of love.

Before I begin my watering gig, Gwyn shows me around so I am clear on what's a weed and what might be a vegetable that's ended up outside its row. And she trains me on the process: turn on the pump, prime it just right and turn it precisely, then say a prayer that it works this time. Water with your thumb over the hose end because there's not enough pressure to use an actual nozzle and fill up the gallon buckets to water the greenhouse plants so you don't get water all over the floor. It takes about half an hour and is fulfilling work.

It's difficult to keep plants growing at high elevations, so what Gwyn does at 8,000 feet is miraculous. The garden thrives here. Even right after the fire, many of the veggies remained, perhaps getting some help from fire hoses.

The act of watering is meditative. My mind is in the moment, on the fresh smell and sound and feel of the water, the splash on the ground, the sights of green spurts, coffee-colored ground, azure sky. Breathing deeply and calmly is a natural byproduct of watering a mountain garden.

My energy level this year is low, and the walk up to Ed and Gwyn's tires me. Some days, the morning and late afternoon waterings are the only exercise I get. I nap a lot.

Gwyn takes regular hikes over to Schultz Canyon and invites me along. I normally love our walks, the chance to chat and just enjoy this amazingness. This year, though, I say no. I could not keep up and I don't want to hold her back. Nor do I honestly feel like it. The hefty climb at the end intimidates me right now, and even the slow steady incline before that seems too much. Mainly I don't want to embarrass myself with having to stop to breathe every 15 steps or so. I worry that breathing the ash has already caused more damage to my lungs.

Planting and monitoring the seedlings and cutting and chipping dead trees takes precedence over just about everything, so mostly we trek to the upper ridge and work. We watch the progress on Harlan and Pat's land next to ours, as trees disappear and mounds of slash—leftover branches mainly—appear.

I used to feel, as we hiked our woods, that we were walking through a poem, the gentle beauty full of rich details that are our reward for paying attention. It's still poetry here, the tone a little darker, but we find hope everywhere, particularly in the aspen groves that are now several feet high and the wildflowers that are crazy beautiful this year.

One day, when everybody else is busy, I decide to walk over the dike alone, needing the solace of a hike. It's usually a 75-minute trek, up a meadow, over the dike, back along the creek.

Gwyn tells me to take the dogs, as she has seen several bears out. So Bella, Ross and I walk through the gate into the neighbors' meadow and up toward the mountain. I go slowly and take a higher-than-usual number of breaks to catch my breath and rest my legs. It's much harder than it has ever been. The dogs run up one hillside, then down and across the meadow to the opposite hill, chasing this, barking at that. I see no wildlife, but they do. I'm glad to see no cows—the herds aren't yet here because the neighbors haven't finished repairing the fences that will keep them in place. Cows scare me—they may not be violent, but good golly they're big. And the sight of a bull sends me up into the brush, my thought being that they will not chase me into trees. So far, so good.

Fun fact: More people are killed in the U.S. by bulls than by bears.

Occasionally, to calm myself around a herd, I think of *The New Yorker* cartoon in which officers break down the door into a room full of cows and yell: "Police! Nobody moo!"

I look to the hilltop for Doc's house, at where the burned hull had been visible last year through the denuded forest. It is completely gone now, as though it had never been there.

The air feels heavy and hard; my lungs continue to struggle.

Last year, at about the same time our fire was burning, California was fighting the Rim Fire in Yosemite National Park, the third largest fire in the state's history. As the fire burned, scientists used NASA aircraft to study the air above it to determine what types of toxins forest fires create. Nor surprising, the air was much like that from a burning oil refinery, emitting methanol, benzene, ozone precursors, and other noxious gases. All this was in microscopic specks the researchers called aerosols, which are especially hazardous to the lungs and heart. Aerosols, which can contain oxidants that cause genetic damage, are concentrated in the fire areas but can drift over long distances into populated areas. This pollution can be worse than that from cars and power plants with pollution controls.

We've been living smack in the middle of these toxic emissions. That my lungs are working as well as they are is a bit of a miracle. Still, a year of rains and winds has certainly cleared up the air by now. Right?

I finally get to the trail over the dike itself. It's normally a fairly easy climb, about 50 feet up through a rock-strewn path. But halfway up, my stomach attacks me out of the blue and I get horribly sick, my head spinning and my stomach churning. I have instant diarrhea and a killer headache. Great. I am a mile away from my family, all of whom are busy and will not notice me missing probably until lunchtime, three hours away. I have my phone, though, so I can call…who? 911, to come pick me up, but where?

I stop, take deep breaths and several gulps of water from my Camelback. Then I look for a tree, which used to be fairly easy in the forest. No way can I wait to get back to my cabin bathroom. But there is no cover, the trees are gone, and I am thankful I am alone and the dogs don't care. I have too few tissues with me, so I have to use leaves for wipes and worry that they're poison oak and I'll get a nasty outbreak and never be able to sit again. And also, they don't work.

I begin to feel better and I try to find a stick to dig a hole and bury my waste, but all I can find are small twigs that snap in the hard ground. I cover it with rocks. Then I slowly walk a few yards down to the creek, wash my hands, then my face, and do my best to clean what the leaves couldn't. I feel like a gross mess.

After about 15 minutes, I resume my walk. Fortunately, it's all downhill from here. I have no idea what was wrong with me, perhaps mental stress pushed to the limit by the physical stress of the walk. I wonder about a heart attack, but my symptoms don't match even the subtle ones for women—I've just written an article about that, so I am aware of silent signs.

Most likely, all the extra toxins in the air got to my lungs. And overall stress.

The longer I walk, the better I feel, and by the time I get close to the cabin, I feel mostly normal. I am still completely disgusting, though, the sweat of the walk adding to my discomfort and potent odor. I'm pretty sure I smell to high heaven.

The thought of a shower at the end keeps me going. Fortunately, neither Ed nor Gwyn is around as I walk by, so I don't need to stop. The dogs wander off to the cottage for water and a rest. And I am finally at the cabin. I walk in and turn into the bathroom, my salvation, my dream for the past half hour.

But Joe has been cleaning our refrigerator vent—it's a gas refrigerator, so keeping the vent pristine is essential. He has been impatiently waiting for me to come home and help him and gets royally pissed that I want to shower rather than helping him right away. He thinks I've been skipping merrily through the woods while he has been working.

I try to tell him that I got sick on my hike, but his stress is too loud to hear mine. I shower, then go to help him and the world does not end because he had to wait. I do think if I had made him smell me for a bit he would have understood.

The walk took me an hour longer than normal. I need to do this more, I tell myself. *Sure, fine*, myself answers.

I have all summer to get fit. Still, I feel like I am losing more weight than normal—we have no scale up here, but my jeans are getting looser. This is likely because of my loss of appetite from stress and depression. But also, the work we are doing is difficult and burns up the calories. That may also account for my lack of energy. I may simply be tired. Physically and mentally.

I grieve the loss of our forests but, more important, I grieve the loss of faith in the future. Fear follows me, tickling my neck with unnerving reminders that this Earth may be indestructible, but its inhabitants are fragile. That we humans may no longer be able to live our lives scurrying around open fields and verdant forests the way we once had. That what had been pockets of peace, like our remote valley, might be most at risk, sort of the canaries in the coal mine because we see the changes first-hand. And for those of us who love the land, that's about as personal as it gets. This is a way of life we wanted for our kids and grandkids. And they may never see it again, certainly not as it had been.

I'm reminded of fires that have given birth to gorgeous new forests, and I hang onto that. But the number of fires recently is unnerving—they've doubled in the past 30 years, burning millions of acres a year, according to research published in 2016 in the *Proceedings of the National Academy of Sciences.* This is change on a serious scale and we've not seen the end of it. We may be just at the beginning.

No matter what I do now, I'm always looking behind me, ahead of me, wondering what's there and what that means to the Rocky Mountains I have known and loved for almost 70 years.

16. Boulders Shifting

We have several days of grueling heat, our thermometers again registering temperatures in the 90s. We get up early to plant and water, then rest in midday and try to catch up on more projects in the evening.

At night, we open as many windows as we think safe. I miss sleeping with windows wide open, the cool mountain air and the sound of the creek lulling us to sleep, oblivious to the creatures roaming about. We now open only those on the highest side of the cabin, which are about five feet off the ground, with no deck. We keep the bathroom window open a few inches. It's tiny, only 12"x18", a bit tight for a bear, I reason. We leave the equally tiny kitchen window open as well, mainly because of our propane refrigerator. Even though it is well vented and we've never had a problem with it, we still feel it's wise to have some outdoor air.

In the mornings, the cabin is cool, so we shut the windows and blinds to trap that air as long as we can. By afternoon, though, it's stuffy, so we begin to strategically open things up. We could use more help than our tiny 8-inch fan, but our solar panels don't pump out enough electricity to support a bigger one.

Joe spends the afternoons in his hammock, hung in a grove of scrub oak right next to the creek. I sweat in the cabin, with the fan and a glass of ice.

We welcome the storm clouds that often come in the late afternoon because they can drop the temperature 20 or more degrees in minutes. But I watch them carefully, remembering the floods, gauging our closeness to the creek.

I monitor rain on the mountain, knowing that whatever falls there will eventually make it down here. And if it falls in buckets there, it will build into an awesome force by the time it reaches us.

Almost a month after we arrive, we see the first serious cloud cover the peak. It's black and mean and it shrouds the mountain completely. We barely get a trickle of rain and by the time we go to bed, the moon is out, and we can see the outline of the entire peak, so we figure the storm has passed.

We crawl into bed and actually use a blanket for a change. Ah, wonderful coolness. I put in my earplugs, but during the night I still hear a little rain hit the roof. I shake off any worry and go back to sleep. I'm tired and this feels so good.

In the morning, it's the smell that gets me first. Rank, dank, and nasty.

I throw an afghan over my nightgown and open the door. Water everywhere. Joe comes up behind me, his hand on my shoulder. Wordlessly, we watch it gush by, over the culvert and through the meadow. Our little bridge, only a few weeks back in place, is again gone—it hangs catawampus in one of the willow trees. Tall batches of grass, pulled up by the roots, scatter and scuttle near the bank, nervously trying to find a way out. Logs and branches bump against one another, thudding their way past.

I call Ed and Gwyn. They have not yet checked the garden—too much water. I tell Ed we slept through the flood and he is flummoxed.

"How could you sleep? It pounded rain all night!"

"Earplugs," I say.

He grunts, reminding me of our dad when I did something he considered dumb, which was quite a bit of the time.

The churning water settles within an hour or so, but the muck remains. We clean out the culvert again and get the bridge out of the tree. Will we rebuild it, or will we wait until right before we have some little ones visit us? Or tell them to stay away from the creek? Or maybe we should just admit defeat and go away ourselves.

We walk up to check on Gwyn's garden and are stopped speechless. The flood got it this time.

After fighting off the waters for a year, the rock wall caved. A carpet of mud is slapped over all the gorgeous plants. Wilted lettuce and broccoli leaves wither in the sludge, onion greens lay flat and broken. The wall is arched forward, pushed out of place by the power of the water. Loose stones are scattered over the ground.

Gwyn is in tears. "This is my baby," she says. I hug her and promise to do whatever we can to help save it. Ed says nothing, just looks on grimly.

They begin rebuilding the wall immediately, adding more fence posts for reinforcement, digging them several feet in the ground, a job that's easier than usual because the ground is moist and pliable.

We wait for the mud to dry a bit then dust it off the plants, going slowly so we don't damage anything further, using our hands and fresh water to remove the dirt and rinse the traumatized plants. Within hours, they respond, reaching cautiously toward the sun.

Together, we save maybe half the garden—most of the lettuce and broccoli and some of the onions. The plants in the greenhouse were fine, so tomatoes and peppers and corn are still growing nicely. And the meadow slowly returns, bits of grass popping back up through the mud, nature's feistiness coming to her rescue.

My feistiness is another matter. I start considering our escape from the next flood, perhaps the big one, the one that will get the cabin. I make sure the car is parked heading down the mountain, toward town. I pack a suitcase so we're ready to go and leave it by the side door. When I don't work on my computer, I put it in its case and leave it in on the dining room table, near the door.

Even small rains turn my heart rate on overdrive, my mind focused only on the potential for more disaster. I take deep breaths, forcing myself to relax, but I am only truly calm when the weather is. I try to pray, but I have never been good at the "God, help me right here and now" sort of missive. Seems unfitting, rude, demanding. I'm more into reflective prayers asking for the tools to help me cope, for strength and wisdom. But I am not feeling circumspect right now. I want God to stop all this and stop it right now.

I've become a cliché: The good Lord willing and the creek don't rise.

A few days later, we wake up to a sunny day, a little cooler than previous mornings, and are feeling energetic, so we decide to walk over the dike. I call Gwyn and ask if she wants to take a break from work and go with us. She's in, but Ed stays behind, as he has already taken his walk with Ross and Bella and has trees to cut. So Joe, Gwyn and I, and the dogs, head up the neighbors' meadow, following the overgrown cow path that winds through grass that is now waist high.

We talk about family, politics, books, health, whatever comes up. Companionable and pleasant, the kind of walk that used to be an almost everyday treat back when our focus was more on time together and less on mountain and personal recovery.

We take break times to look around at the surrounding hills and down the valley, toward our places, and the plateaus to the east. We can see for probably 30 miles before the landscape melts into sky.

The hill to our right is a continuation of our ridge and is a total burn; the fire came down farther here, almost to the meadow. There's no buffer of healthy trees between the meadow and the ridge, as on our land. To our left is the dike, a rise of a few hundred feet, covered with live stands of aspen that create a gorgeous green screen hiding the blackness behind.

We climb over the dike, an easier hike for me this time, which is encouraging. Maybe my health is not totally shot. The mountain looks over our shoulders. At the bottom of the dike we come to the creek, ready to cross it.

Or not. We stop and stare at what's before us. The creek is four times wider than it had been, far too wide for our usual jump across. Worse, though, and more terrifying, are all the boulders that have tumbled off the mountain and now fill the creek. Dozens of them, two to three feet across, building a natural wall of rock. Who knows how far these things have rolled? I imagine them roaring down in a torrent of water. Then I imagine them going farther, another mile, to our cabin and into our little hideaway.

It's not likely the rocks would make it that far, as the terrain is much flatter from now on, so there would be less force to move the boulders toward us. A week ago, though, I would not have imagined them this far. Dave had told us last year that rocks were falling along Bear Creek and into the scout camp. Regular flooding caused the camp to close again this year after only a couple of weeks.

"Imagine how this happened," Gwyn finally says, surveying the damage.

"When do you think that was?" Joe asks.

"It had to be the last flood. I was here right before that," I say, envisioning boulders raining down apocalyptically.

I'm the only one with a walking stick, so we share it as we straddle rocks to get through the water to the other side. There's mud and dried grass all along the path, signs that the flood had covered most of the little valley we're now in.

"Kind of terrifying," I say, hoping the others will disagree. I want my reaction to seem overblown to others. I want it to be a personal failing, not a truth.

Instead, Gwyn says, "It is."

"Yep," Joe says simply.

We follow the narrow creek valley for about half a mile before it opens up to the larger meadow, which is usually calm, bucolic, the normal creek about three feet wide, bubbling through thick mountain grasses and over water-worn rocks.

Now the water has ripped a jagged trench through the earth, a six-foot drop of fresh dirt and exposed grass roots over which water washes wildly. Rocks are scattered carelessly at the bottom.

Joe climbs down to investigate. It's taller than he is, and he's an inch shy of six feet. The chasm continues for a few hundred feet until the creek again settles at its normal stage, just a sliver of water through the grass, which is now matted and littered with tree branches, logs, and small rocks. The strength of the water that did this is unimaginable.

We just keep walking. There's nothing to say.

It's just a few minutes from here to Ed and Gwyn's and we head to the cottage porch for a break. Gwyn calls for Ed, who is in the house cleaning up, to join us. He and Gwyn settle in the granny rockers, Joe and I are in plastic chairs. Gwyn hands me a Diet Coke and gets one for herself. Ed sips Constant Comment tea, and Joe drinks the tea he brought with him in his water bottle. The hummingbirds screech and dart among the three feeders hanging from the roof.

We tell Ed about the boulders.

"Have you looked up there lately?" he asks, pointing toward the peak.

"I look there all the time," I answer.

We stare at the gorges at the top of the mountain, where rocks and dirt have been routed out, each crevasse probably 20 feet deep.

Ed passes his binoculars and each of us takes a closer look at the bare mountain, acres of grey trees that just look sadder and more desolate closer up. All the way up to tree line. Acres of dead.

We hand the binoculars back and sit silently in the shade of the roof, quiet except for the gentle rocking of the chairs and the clatter of the birds.

17. The Bear

The next rains are mild, and the creek remains calm. Water flows politely by the cabin. We find muddy bear prints on our porch every morning. Once we notice a print about five feet up, on the wall. He must be chasing bugs, we think, and dismiss the intrusion. He's outside. We're inside. There's a cabin between us. All is fine.

We joke about the rain and the creek. I tell Ed that, despite long rains the night before, the creek did not rise at all.

"Yes," he says. "It didn't even raise its voice."

Still, I watch. The suitcase remains by the door, the computer in its case on the table.

Joe tries a new recipe of potatoes, broccoli, and cheese with generous garlic and spices. It cooks on the grill slowly, sending aromas out across the valley for more than an hour. It's delicious and we enjoy it on the deck, with a salad and a glass of wine.

At about 9 p.m., the rains start, fairly heavy, but not a downpour. We get our searchlight out and point it at the creek. It's moving fast, but well within its banks. Five minutes later, it's a little higher, but still in its banks. We watch a movie, getting up during lulls in the screen action to check the water level. Still in its banks. The rain peters out through the evening and finally, at nearly midnight, it stops. We can see the creek going down. We put the searchlight away, shut out the lights, and crawl into bed. It's cool and calm out and we're exhausted. I'm so tired I don't even need the earplugs.

The window next to our bed is open, as are the ones in the bathroom and kitchen. We can feel the breeze waft over our bed. So relaxing. So good.

We sleep soundly, restfully.

Then a crash, a thud, a rustle. We both jump up and look at the front door. Through its window, I can see the unmistakable shape—giant head, jaunty ears. A bear at the front door. Fortunately, it is safety glass and the door is shut and locked. Still, he must have clawed the screen door because he is right against the glass, probably thinking about next moves. He seems to be squatting on his haunches, and about half of the top of his head is visible.

"Shoo!" I yell. "Shoo! Get away!"

"Get away!" Joe shouts. "Go!"

We are oddly complacent, assuming he will just leave. We're still in bed, sitting up, yelling at a bear. There have been times when we've had more fun in bed.

The bear moves away from the door, but we hear another crash on the side deck. He's knocked the grill over. The smell of last night's aromatic casserole is probably what lured him, told him he would find food here.

Bears have never bothered the grill before, and this one discovers why: nothing there. Joe does not cook directly on the grates; he uses a pan he then brings inside, so no food stays on the grill.

We crawl tentatively out of the safety of our bed and move cautiously to the side door. We look out its window. The bear looks right back at us. He's less than a foot away from us.

We continue shouting at him. I get a pan and a spoon and begin banging. It doesn't work.

He's still staring at us through the glass even as we yell at him and beat our pots. Seeing a bear this close is a stunning reminder that the beasts we share this mountainside with are massive creatures. His head feels the size of both of ours combined. And I can see the muscles working in legs three times the thickness of my arm. So, yes, big. With sharp teeth and claws and strong jaws.

He turns slowly toward the bathroom, then stands up on two legs and puts his giant paws on the bathroom screen. I realize the window is open, and I rush to shut it. If he could get a paw inside, he could rip it out of its frame and get in.

He and I are now face-to-face, just six inches apart, separated by a flimsy window screen. I can hear him breathing. Steady breaths through his nose; he doesn't sound all that aggressive or excited, but I have never been within a foot of a bear's head before, so I am in no position to assess.

He's big. And he is right there.

As quickly as I can, I slam the window in his face and lock it. I can no longer hear him breathe, but he stands there on the deck, looking back at me through yellow eyes.

He pushes back from the window and lands on the deck on all fours, then moves to the front door. We follow him with our ineffective noisemakers. We've stopped yelling—we've tried to be the alphas in this scenario and the bear doesn't seem to really care. Or believe us. He patrols the deck, back and forth, back and forth, back and forth and, finally, finally saunters away, toward the shed, as the sun starts to rise.

We watch his giant rump swing from side to side as he waddles off into the distance and out of sight.

Surprisingly, we both crawl back into bed and fall asleep for another three hours. The sun coming up somehow makes me feel safer, as though we would not be attacked in broad daylight. Certainly bears know that.

· · ·

When we awake, we go out and survey the damage. The front screen door hangs off one bent hinge, torn and twisted. This is the door that had been broken for years, the door Joe had finally fixed just a week ago. It is done for.

"Goddamn it!" Joe mutters.

"Guess you should have waited to fix it," I joke.

He scowls audibly.

The bear hit the window so hard the door's safety glass has an imprint of the screen. The bathroom screen has two long rips where his paws landed. The grill is upside down on the ground a couple feet from the deck.

Gwyn stops by on her morning walk and looks at the damage. "Were you terrified?" she asks. Interestingly, we had simply been in action mode and weren't that frightened at all at the time. I think about standing in front of the bear and shutting the window and I think, *Wow. Huh.*

The dogs sniff excitedly all around the deck and grill, smelling the bear. Ross takes a special interest, pacing from one window to the next, then to the grill and back again, his snout twitching in overtime to catch the scent. Gwyn tries to get him back to the road for the walk.

"Come, Ross!"

"Ross! Come!"

"Ross! Come!"

Finally, he runs to the road. More bears there? Maybe. He lopes excitedly. Life is such an adventure for Ross. Bella follows slowly, with practiced nonchalance. Bears are not her job.

Joe and I decide to go to Trinidad to see if we can find an electric fence like Harlan and Pat's. First, we stop at their house and check out their design. They have fenced the screened portions of their porch, but their door, of metal and glass, is not electrified. Otherwise they would have to unhook the fence every time they go in.

In our case, the bear went right to the door, so we feel the door would have to be electrified as well.

"They haven't bothered us since we built the fence," Harlan reminds us.

Pat shows us the strands of wire that wrap across the porch, about 18 inches apart, to catch the bear at whatever level he tries to reach. It makes sense for a screened porch, but I'm having trouble seeing it work on the cabin.

Harlan and Pat walk us out to their gravel driveway, down to the road, and continue chatting, offering encouragement and advice. We wave at them as we drive off, down toward the switchback, past Pearl's and off to the interstate toward Trinidad.

We have two shopping choices: True Value Hardware and Big R Farm and Ranch Supply. The hardware store doesn't have what we need, and Big R only has small fences, none that would keep a bear away. We begin looking at installation options and realize this is going to be clumsy and difficult, at best. Ineffective, at worst.

The salesman at Big R is helpful and knowledgeable and tells us he makes sure he takes all his bird feeders in at night, so they don't lure bears. Bears have never bothered our feeders, nor have they bothered Ed and Gwyn's, and they have about five of them. Still, there was that footprint on the wall that I thought was made by a bear looking for bugs. Could have been reaching for the hummingbirds. Could have been trying to get to the syrup in the feeder.

Stymied by the fence, we go to the coffee shop to check the Internet for solutions. Bird feeders should be at least 10 feet above the ground, we read. Ours are two feet below that. OK, so we bring those in at night.

Also, experts say bears are deterred by cloths drenched in ammonia, Lysol, or Pine-Sol and hung on doors and windows. Motion sensor lights might scare them away. Unwelcome mats of nails, sharp side up and two inches apart, keep them from getting in. One site suggests keeping your car alarm ready, as that noise can scare the big guys. We discount the unwelcome mats for now because if we put them in front of the door, we'd somehow have to get over them ourselves. Plus, they sound mean. We buy motion detector lights, Pine-Sol, and ammonia.

Hidden in the research are data on the reality of living with bears. Bears seldom kill people, but it has happened. According to Laura Pritchett's well-researched *Great Colorado Bear Stories*, three people have been killed by bears in Colorado since the Colorado Parks and Wildlife began tracking deaths in 1969. According to the North American Bear center site, dangerous bears are unusual, and they are often motivated by fear or hunger. Bears usually come out the losers in interactions with humans, and their "crime" often is just trying to survive.

Joe puts the lights on the front deck; he sets them to flash, hoping the strobe light effect is more frightening than a static light. He takes down the mangled screen and replaces it with the storm window that came with the screen door. Maybe the Plexiglas will at least turn the bear off; it's been stored for at least a decade under the cabin and is clouded and stained, but we don't care how it looks.

That night, I put the car alarm on the table, with a flashlight. I slather the Pine-Sol on some old rags and tack them to the window frames on the deck, then I spray the deck and the door molding with the stuff. I have to wash my hands multiple times to get the smell off.

Know why bears don't like the smell of Pine-Sol?

Because they have noses.

The lights are a nuisance; everything sets them off. Hummingbirds, mice, chipmunks. And each time, I rush to the deck to make sure nothing is there. *Breathe in, breathe out.* It's working. No bears. No flood. *Breathe in. Breathe out.*

Then, again at 5 a.m., I hear Ross barking in the road behind the cabin. From the sound, he must be fairly close, a few dozen feet or so. And then I hear a deep-throated growl.

It takes me a while before I realize I am hearing bear sounds. I have never heard a peep from a bear up here. No bear has even opened its mouth near me, not even our night visitor.

Clearly, though, this is dog versus bear. Ross is a big guy, but he's still only about a quarter the size of a bear. He is, however, fearless. Or, as it sometimes seems, witless.

He barks and snarls. The bear growls and snarls.

Go home, Ross, I pray.

But on and on it goes, for about a year and a half, it seems.

As I lie there listening, my heart begins to pump faster and faster, my breath gets shorter. I feel clammy. I focus on deep breathing, but the sounds on the road are impossible to ignore.

Breathe in, breathe out.

Woof. Growl. Snarl. Not sure which is which, who is who. Two alpha males having it out on the road. They are getting louder. They are getting closer.

Joe sleeps through it all.

Finally, it's ominously quiet, no dog, no bear, just the peace of the mountain. I hope Ross is fine, that he has just gone home, and the bear has moved on. Certainly, I tell myself, I would have heard signs of distress otherwise.

And then the motion lights go off, and it looks like a police car has pulled up to the cabin. The flashing sets me off again. My heart thuds, my breathing quickens. I gasp for air. I don't even have to see the bear; I just know he is there. He is probably pretty excited after his argument with Ross. The lights keep flashing. This is more than birds or mice or chipmunks.

"I think he's back," I tell Joe, who is still sound asleep. He doesn't respond. "The bear. I think he's back," I repeat, nudging Joe to awaken him.

"Huh, who?" Joe mutters groggily, pulling the blanket more tightly under his neck.

"The bear," I say.

Joe sighs and groans, sitting up halfway, blinking himself awake.

"I think he's at the door again," I say.

Joe finally sits up completely and sees the lights on the deck.

That wakes him up. He exhales loudly, in frustration. "You don't think it's hummingbirds, huh?" I think he's joking and he's about a thousand miles away from being funny.

"It's the bear," I say.

We get up and go to the door and there he is again, pacing the deck, apparently undeterred by the Pine Sol smell and by the light glinting off his furry back.

"Shoo!" I yell. "Shoo! Get away!"

"Get away!" Joe shouts. "Go!"

It's like we have a script. The bear shrugs it off and walks from the front door to the side, sniffing, pacing.

"Shoo!"

He paces.

Then I remember the car alarm. I reach over to the table and hit it.

The bear literally jumps and, in an instant, hightails it off the deck, toward the shed and out of sight.

Wow! Who knew? The car alarm worked. If only we had thought of that the first time. Maybe he now thinks of this as the scary cabin with the monster with bright blinking eyes and a blaring voice. Let's hope.

We don't go back to sleep.

The bear left quickly, which logically should have calmed me. It didn't. I focus instead on the fact that he will most certainly come again. He tried to get in once, so will likely try again. He's not giving up.

I replay the sounds of his fight with Ross in the road.

Breathe in, breathe out.

Then, in the nanosecond it takes for me to assess my threats, I envision another fire, another flood, this time with water and rocks crashing through our windows. Another bear. The same bear again.

Breathe, breathe, breathe.

We have an early breakfast and watch the sunrise. Ed drives by on Alice, heading down the road, probably going up the ridge today. Ross and Bella are with him. Phew. Ross is obviously unhurt. We wave.

We decide to go up to water our trees in the cool of the morning. We'll keep busy. We intend to stop at the shed to get the 50-pound bag of dry dog food we've had stored there for a year. We bought it right after the fire to feed the bears, one of our more insane moves. We knew the bears would be hungry and we figured it would be safe if we sprinkled food for them on the ridge far from the cabin.

But the bears weren't interested. The kibble stayed on the ground until the rains turned it into sawdust. We used only about a tenth of the bag and stored the rest in the shed, another insane move.

Harlan told us it's a bad idea to feed bears, no matter how far away, and we know he's right. But if it's unsafe to have food elsewhere in the forest, it's even less safe to have it in a shed right by our cabin. We plan to once again spread it on the ridge and if it turns to dust again, so be it. At least it will be out of the shed.

We load up our water tank, watering cans and jugs, water bottles and snack bars, hats and gloves and clippers. Then we jump into Mr. Green Jeans. As we drive about 100 feet past the shed, Joe says, "Oh, no!"

"What?"

"We forgot the dog food."

I sigh. "Together you'd think we'd at least have one decent brain."

"Should we go back?"

"No, it's been there for a year; we can take it up tomorrow."

We continue on our way to get the trees watered. They look healthy; so far all are still alive. Maybe they'll keep growing, maybe they won't. We can only do what we can.

Knowing I would be planting in our scorched woods, I had dressed accordingly: socks stained gray from previous work; dusty, ashy boots; a black shirt I'd bought at a resale shop in town. I'm not sure why I chose khaki pants, though, because a few minutes on the ridge and they are patterned with black lines where I'd run into burned shrubs. It's impossible to walk through the woods even a few feet without being slapped with charcoal sticks.

Watering is a long process and we're exhausted and ready for lunch when we get back. The afternoon is cooler than it has been, so Joe enjoys the hammock and I read and do some work on the computer. We have a salad and a martini for dinner, eating outside, watching the stars come up, until it's too cool to stay out.

The kitchen and bathroom windows are locked shut, but we still have the one open by our bed, and it brings in pleasantly chilly air. So it should be an easy night for sleeping. But when I hit the pillow, my mind goes to the bear and my heart starts thudding again. Just one thought of him and I am off.

Thud, thud, thud.

Breathe in, breathe out.

I remember my premonition and again see the bear in my mind walking past our bed. My heart beats faster. What would we do if he broke in? The cabin is one big room and we would have nowhere to go. I sit up and try to breathe. It's just stress, I remind myself. *Breathe*. My heart slows again but my mind is on full alert. I imagine the bear at the door, at the window. I give up and take an Ambien—I have a prescription I seldom use, but this is a good night for an exception. It works, and I fall asleep.

I awake again, reflexively, at 5 a.m. Alert, listening. But there's nothing. I fall back asleep and awake at 7 to a beautiful sunny morning. We enjoy breakfast on the deck and plan our day. We'll cut some weeds on the ridge, so Joe heads to the shed for the clippers.

He's there for quite a while but comes back empty handed.

"Well, the bear got the dog food," he says simply.

"Ohhh," I sigh. The bear is not going to leave us alone. He's hungry and he knows we have food. It's unfair, terrifying, heartbreaking.

I go down to the shed and see the window ripped completely out, frame and all. We had opened it in the afternoon and forgotten it. Dog food pellets are sprinkled all over the floor, but the 50-pound bag is gone. We never find it. Interestingly, the shed is less a mess than you might expect, probably because the only edible thing in there was the dog food, and that's all the bear was after.

"OK," I say, "That's it." We need help.

I look up the name of the conservation officer in Huerfano County, intending to ask for advice and information and perhaps get some perspective. Maybe he can even calm us down a bit. The woman who answers when I call says she'll give our local officer the message and maybe he can bring up some bear deterrents, specifically mentioning the unwelcome mats.

I wait for his return call while Joe boards up the shed window. It's early afternoon before the call comes. I explain our problem and the officer—I'll call him Tom—says he'll be up to see how he can help us, but he'll also bring a trap in case he feels he needs to catch the bear.

We assume the trap is a stretch, just a precaution, that we'll learn how to better deflect this guy's attention. It's late afternoon before the truck pulls up, with the Colorado Parks and Wildlife logo, pulling a metal cage the size of a small U-Haul.

He's a young man who seems to know his job. We tell him our problem and show him the damage. He looks at the bathroom window. "He's a young guy," he says. "Probably no more than two. Most likely lost his mother in the fire or over the winter and doesn't know how to take care of himself yet."

"He seemed so big," I say.

"Well, he is. But he's still small for a bear."

And, Tom says, he's a hungry bear. It's late July, time to get ready for hibernation; at this time of year, Tom says, bears can consume as many as 20,000 calories a day to store for their long sleep. Whoa. I wonder how many calories are in an adult human.

Adding to the problem, he reminds us, is that the fire burned many of the bushes and trees that provide the bears' natural diet—berries and acorns. Not much out there to eat.

"We've been getting a lot of calls the past couple of days," he says. Lots of bear problems.

"Are any from around here?" I ask.

He looks around at our wilderness and laughs: "There *isn't* anything around here."

Fair enough.

"Do you have a gun?" he asks.

"No."

"Not even a rifle?"

"No."

"If you did, I could give you some rubber bullets to scare him off," he says. I imagine an instance in which I could honestly, logically, shoot at the bear. Through the window? Once he's inside the cabin? As he retreats?

"If you just hit him in the rump with a rubber bullet, chances are he wouldn't return," Tom says.

Chances are….

"Well, we don't have a gun," Joe says.

I mention that my brother and his wife live nearby.

"Do they have a gun?" Tom asks hopefully.

"No, they don't have a gun either."

"All right," Tom shrugs. Matter closed, even though we're pretty sure it's not to his liking. "Let's see the house." *House* is a charitable term, I think.

We walk around the outside of the cabin so he can assess how a bear could get in. The bathroom is a target, he says, because of all the smells—carrot shampoo, citrus soap, and lavender lotion in ours. Bears have no idea that, if they get into this stash, they will be washing out their mouths with soap.

Good to know.

We walk on.

"That's the dining room?" he asks as we look at the table through the window.

"Yes," I say. *Room* is pretty generous, but it is a dining place; no need to parse the details here.

We walk to the far end of the deck. "And that's the office?" he asks, looking in at my desk.

"Yes," I again reply, wondering if he comprehends how small this place is.

We walk off the deck and around the corner. "And so this is the bedroom," he says, looking in at our bed.

"Sure."

"A bear could get in every one of these windows," he says.

"Even this one?" I ask, pointing at the bottom frame of the bedroom window, which is about nose height on me, and I am 5'10".

"Of yeah," he shrugs. "It would be easy."

He was supposed to make me feel better. Instead, I am feeling increasingly at risk. Information does not feel like power in this case. He suggests boarding up the windows as a precaution, meaning we would be inside a locked, airless cabin.

"You could put some pots and pans outside the bedroom window—that would wake you up if he tried to get in there," he adds. But this would be just like the strobe lights—a cause of additional worry. If even a skunk wandered by and tripped it, I'd be terrified. And it would not keep the bear out.

We go back to the side deck and look down at the trap.

"He'll keep coming back," Tom says. "He's hungry and he smells food here." Trapping him, Tom says, is a wise option.

"So would you settle him elsewhere?" I ask.

"No," he answers simply. "We don't do that anymore. It's too dangerous. He's likely to try to break in someplace else. We'd be liable if he did."

He'll be "put down," Tom says.

I exhale, blowing my frustration through my mouth. The bear doesn't deserve this. He's just hungry. He's trying to live his normal, natural life, while humans have intruded on his land. And it's humans who have caused the climate crisis he's fighting. This is on us, not him, yet he is the loser.

We thought we had done what we should to live in the wild, to keep us and the bears safe. But that was when there was food in the forest. If he'd had his mom around longer, maybe he'd have better survival skills. If he'd had food, maybe he would be safe without his mother. Maybe, maybe, maybe.

Joe and I look at one another silently. His eyes, so expressive, are deeply sad. I am again on the verge of tears.

If we agree to the trap, we will be complicit in killing a bear. I try to tell myself that this is not my choice, that I would do what I could to keep him away safely, but I no longer see any options for doing that. Nature is full of injustices, but this seems the most unjust version of them all. Not natural, manmade.

And, Tom adds, there is a good chance he will just get increasingly aggressive and be a risk to others.

It seems the only thing we could have done differently—other than not being here in the first place—is buying a gun. And I can't imagine the level of training I would need to be safe shooting at a bear.

Bear encounters are more common in nearby cities because of the plentiful sources of food—garbage, fruit trees, bird feeders. But they feel more frightening here. In town, you can call the sheriff. It would take a patrol car from Walsenburg, our closest town, 45 minutes to get up here, if one would come at all. But that's part of our decision to live in the wilderness and, for most of the two decades we've been here, we've had no cause before to question what we've done and how we've done it. We wanted to live at least part of the time in nature yet keep a small footprint, this remains the best choice.

Tom explains the process. He puts fresh meat in the back of the cage as a lure; when the bear wanders in for the bait, the reinforced steel door will shut. The cage has bars on all sides for air, I suppose to keep the beast comfortable until they kill it. Or, maybe, reasonably calm after it's trapped.

Joe and I look at one another again and then nod in reluctant agreement.

"OK," he says.

"OK," I agree.

I ask if the cage is a risk to dogs, thinking of Ross and Bella. "It's usually too high," Tom says. "And dogs tend to stay away." Then he looks around, an air of hope again in his voice, and asks, "Do you have a dog?"

"No, my brother has two."

"Maybe you could borrow one for the night," he suggests. I think of Ross's altercation with the bear two nights before and imagine him growling and barking in the cabin while the bear snarls and snorts outside.

I shake my head. "No, I don't think that will work."

"OK," Tom says, then walks down to his truck and pulls a slab of bacon from a cooler. He heats it up with a hand lighter. I smell it immediately. The bear will as well.

He stands for a while, hands casually on his hips, checking the cage, then looks across at the meadow and down at the creek. Finally, he comes up to the deck and gives us his number to call if there is a bear in the trap in the morning. He wishes us luck, jumps into his truck, turns around in the meadow, and heads back to town.

It's dusk by now.

"I'm not staying here tonight," I tell Joe.

When I researched bear deterrents, I saw photos of cabins trashed by bears, of rips bears had made right through siding and into a house. I remember the gash a bear made through the metal of the trailer Ed and Gwyn had lived in while we were building up here.

"But Tom's set the trap. The bear will go there," Joe argues.

"Before or after the cabin?" I ask.

Joe can reason all he wants, but the fact is, I am not staying here for the night. I already feel shaky at the thought, my hands sweaty. I call Ed and Gwyn and ask them to check the cage in the morning. Then we take our suitcase, already packed, and my computer, climb into Mr. Green Jeans and leave.

We get a room in a motel on the outskirts of Walsenburg, a plain Mom and Pop kind of place that gets good ratings. I feel the need to share and tell the young man who is checking us in that we're here because there's a problem bear at our cabin.

"Are you the people with the bear cage?" he asks. "We saw the game warden drive through town with it."

"Yeah," I say sadly, "We're the people with the bear cage."

The room is simple but clean. We shower, then have a light dinner at Corine's across the street. We get online, enjoying the Wi-Fi after our slow mountain Internet, and watch our travel standby: HGTV.

When we've had our fill of the *Property Brothers*, we crawl into bed. I figure I'll feel safe inside the motel, but as I rest my head on the pillow, my heart begins its little panic dance and I can feel my hands shake. It feels like I have a small, wild animal trying to break out of my chest. My own little bear caught in a trap.

Breathe in, breathe out. The tiny beast continues to jump inside my rib cage.

Breathe in, breathe out. No luck.

I take an Ambien and finally fall asleep.

18. Warning: Do Not Crack

I call Gwyn as soon as I wake up in the morning, hoping the trap is full and Tom can come get the bear.

"It's empty," she says. "No bear."

My shoulders slump and tears fill my eyes. No luck. No bear. He's still roaming.

"Your cabin looks fine, though," she assures us.

She says the bear had been around—Ross was prancing and growling throughout the night until they finally let him out. He barked a few times and that was it. In the past, that was fine, normal. Now, though, this threat feeds into my fear. I puff air to release tension, but my throat constricts and sends me into a nervous cough.

We return to the mountain for breakfast, driving by the empty cage. I place the suitcase by the door and dump the computer on the table, ready to go again.

We eat our cereal and blueberries then sit and sip our tea on the deck.

I keep thinking of what's the best thing to do next, arguing with myself: *I want to go. You should stay. I'm scared. Get over it. I want to go.*

"I'm ready to go home," I finally say, making a commitment out loud.

"For good?" Joe asks.

"For the year," I say. We'd be leaving six weeks earlier than planned.

"Are you sure?" Joe asks.

We sip quietly, looking at the mountain. I don't want to leave all this, but I know I can't stay.

"Yes," I finally answer. "I just don't feel safe." Lordy, how I hate to say that, but it is true. I feel at risk. I am beginning to question whether I—we, any of us—belong here.

"Oh, I think we're fine, but if you're worried, it might be best to leave," he says.

"Yes. I am worried." I sigh.

"Right away?" he asks.

"Today," I answer. I don't like this decision, but I don't hesitate in making it. It is the right thing to do, no matter how lousy it makes me feel.

I call Tom and tell him we're leaving. He says he'll bring new bait for the trap later this evening, but that we don't need to be there. Ed and Gwyn will check the trap in the morning and call him with news.

Gwyn stops by on her way for a walk. Ross comes first, happily sniffing at me, then moving on, not wanting to miss his exciting day: *A walk! A walk!* Bella again barely acknowledges us, just stays on the road, facing ahead. Neither bothers the cage.

Gwyn suggests I get anti-anxiety medicine. But this place has always been its own relaxation drug. Does it make sense to be here if I need medication to handle it? We have a lovely home in Iowa, without fires, floods, and bears. Staying here right now just makes no sense.

I ask her if she'll check the trap again.

"Sure," she says with only slight hesitation. She is an animal lover, so a trapped bear would be a sad sight to her; still, she understands my fear. And I know she, not Ed, will be the one to look inside the trap. He will not want anything to do with capturing a creature like this.

Joe goes down to the shed and brings back pieces of board to cover the doors and windows. It's painted glossy red, left over from when he replaced the sides of a garden cart Phyllis had given us. Festive. We normally just lock the doors and windows, pull down the shades and leave. Ed and Gwyn stay up here until snow comes, so they keep an eye on the cabin. And Harlan and Pat monitor the road—nobody can get here without going in front of their house. When they leave, they lock the gate.

But we've always been worried only about two-legged intruders in the past.

Joe shows me how he plans to place the boards. I really do not care. And what do I know about boarding up a cabin?

Later, Ed drives up on Alice, stops, and comes to the deck. He sits next to me on the side deck, on our boot box. We're right beneath the bathroom window; the bear's paw prints are still on the siding behind us.

He looks down at the cage suspiciously, a sterile metal block in the grassy meadow. I can still smell a bit of the bacon.

"The dogs were here and didn't seem interested in it," I say.

"Good." He's succinct, clipped. I'm not sure how to interpret this. Worry? Annoyance? Probably both. Worried that bears are now a threat, annoyed that they might have to pay the ultimate price for it.

And tired. Ed is obviously exhausted. The work of healing the mountain has done him in.

"So, what are you going to do?" he asks, looking over at Joe, who has begun nailing the boards to the side windows.

"We're leaving," I say. "Maybe I'm overreacting, but...." I don't mention the panic attacks. They're such a weakling response. I should be more of a trouper, chin up, all that. But I can't do it. I just want out. I want to stop the constant worry.

"Do you need anything?" he asks. *Therapy*, I think.

"No, I'll call the forest service guy, ask him about the trap. He suggested we board the place up."

"Sounds inviting," Ed says.

"Yeah. He also said we should borrow one of your dogs."

"You can have Ross," he laughs.

I laugh tepidly, thinking of Ross and the bear in the road.

Phew.

We have too much to say, so we're silent.

"When do you plan to leave?" he asks.

"Later this afternoon."

"We'll stop by before you go," he says.

Joe takes a break from shuttering the cabin to bring me stacks of empty apple boxes from the shed. I clean the kitchen and bathroom down to the bare cabinets, packing everything that might have a scent—all shampoo, soap, spices, pasta, tea. The mound of dirty laundry grows in the middle of the floor, as I add towels, bedding, curtains, and work clothes. I pack my bag for an overnight stay at Phyllis's in Pueblo and, perhaps, another on the way home to Iowa.

We keep an eye on the weather, as clouds build up all around us. The valley is steeped in dark clouds, a sign that the high plains along Interstate 25 are getting rain. But so far, we're dry. I check the NOAA forecast on the computer—an 80 percent chance of heavy rain and flooding. We rush to outrun it.

All this with a backdrop of Joe pounding boards over the windows, blocking the sunlight. The cabin is cave-like, no longer our bright, airy refuge.

I put pillows into the cedar cabinet and in plastic bags in the wicker chest at the foot of our bed. I tuck a sheet over the mattress and another over the couch. We don't have a problem with mice, but I want to protect against the hordes of dead flies that greet us every spring.

This is a homemade cabin, crafted by amateurs, so it has tiny cracks all over the place. Flies don't need much of an opening and, once they're in, they breed quickly and in great numbers. One female can lay as many as 500 eggs, which turn into larvae then pupae and finally into adult flies within 7 days. A day or two after they hatch, they are ready to mate. But they need food to survive and they don't have much in the cabin, just a few bugs and crumbs we inevitably leave behind. They die in our windowsills and bathtub and drawers and basically everywhere.

Winterizing the plumbing goes blessedly smoothly. All the knobs that are supposed to shut and those that are supposed to open do so easily and the antifreeze flows through the system exactly where and how it should. Ed and Gwyn come down with the dogs just as I am changing into clean clothes for the trip. I give them a stamped manila envelope for our mail, which we had arranged to be forwarded from Iowa until the middle of September. We will go to the post office in Des Moines and change it back to our address, but we're likely to miss a few things in the process.

"Everything packed?" Joe asks, hammer in hand.

I walk through the dark and empty space, checking the cabinets again for anything with an odor. "Yep."

He shuts the front door, locks it, boards it up, then goes across the deck to do the same on the side door. The cabin looks like an abandoned shack, like a place unloved, left behind. It reminds me of the deserted houses we used to tour in Victor and Cripple Creek in the 1950s, when both were ghost towns and before they became gambling towns or vacation destinations. They were a little like this. One even had decades-old dirty dishes still on the table, ratty linens on the bed. Those folks left in even a bigger hurry than we did. We always speculated that they were bank robbers who were just a step ahead of the law. Maybe Bonnie and Clyde. I now am the one running, just a step ahead of a bear. Or a flood. Or a fire.

The cabin is officially deserted, and we turn away from it, hug Ed and Gwyn and head out. As usual, I have sacks of garbage on my lap. We drive past the bear trap but look the other way.

We stop to tell Harlan and Pat goodbye.

"Not going to wait it out?" Harlan says.

"We're not sure what we'd be waiting for…or with," I say. We explain that our one-room cabin feels terribly exposed, that we'd have nowhere to go if a bear broke in. And because our two doors are so close to one another (bad planning), if he broke into one, we couldn't get out the other.

I feel I am over explaining. I feel guilty, somehow at fault in all this. Not up to mountain life standards.

We drive by Pearl's and think about stopping, but we should have called beforehand. We wave, knowing that she often watches cars go by. We drop the garbage into the dumpster and head down the gravel road, past the neighbor's alfalfa patch, along the pond that's formed with all this new rain, up to the turnoff to the east, slowing for random cows wandering the road, past the old goat barn that became a dance hall and is now storage, telling it all a silent goodbye.

I realize we haven't even seen Dave this trip or talked to him at all. We're all cocooning a bit, I think.

Interstate 25 is wet with rains we must have just missed; scores of rainbows color the sky. They are clear as glass, yet look solid, as though they grow from one arroyo into another, like we could drive up to them and ride right through a prism.

It all looks fresh and glorious. A new beginning, the resurrection we had hoped for. I should feel sad for leaving this wonder, I think, but I am just numb; the protective coating over my emotions comes with a warning: *Do not crack.*

• • •

We meet Phyllis at Jorge's Sombrero in Pueblo, which is about a mile from where we grew up on Spruce Street. She's already at a booth, sipping an iced tea. I look at her tea, shrug and order a margarita. It tastes better than anything has a right to taste. I think of having another but know two drinks is always a mistake. I savor this one and the relaxation it brings.

We have a pleasant dinner—only my second enchiladas with green chili for the year—then head to Phyllis's to talk a bit more over homemade peach pie. I do yoga before bed, hoping that and the margarita will calm me, but when I lie down, I hear the usual noises—dogs barking, doors slamming—and my breathing quickens, my heartbeat swells. I toss for about an hour then finally pop half an Ambien. As I drift away, I have brief worries that I will face some Ambien-induced craziness and wake up in the middle of the night to drive the car up Pikes Peak or eat the rest of the pie.

But I awake with no crumbs on my pillow; the car keys are where I left them.

Phyllis and I are sipping coffee and Joe is having his morning tea when Gwyn calls early the next morning.

"There's a bear in the trap!" she says.

I am happy for success, unhappy for what it means. Phyllis and Joe cheer in the background. "I hope it's the right one," I say.

"It has to be," she says. Then asks, "So are you coming back now?"

I laugh. We've made a pretty irrevocable decision to leave and the bear was only the final cause of my stress. The risk of flood remains. And the possibility of other bears. If the one that was caught was part of the pair we had seen in the meadows and hills, the other one is still around.

• • •

We've requested a small breakfast, just yogurt and fruit, so that is what Phyllis serves us. Also, French toast and bacon. Joe wolfs it all down. I have small servings of everything, because it is all delicious—Phyllis is a marvelous cook—but I still have a queasy stomach and an 800-mile drive ahead of me.

Fed and watered, we leave Pueblo in mid-morning, stopping to get fresh Pueblo chili peppers at a stand outside of town. Workers sweat over three huge metal roasters that cook the peppers, while the sharp, pungent, slightly sweet smell tickles our noses and slightly burns our eyes. Farm trucks drive up, their open beds overflowing with shiny green chilis. We buy a few pounds of fresh peppers plus some pepper jelly and a potica, a Slovene walnut bread, for neighbors who have watched our house and watered our plants.

Somewhere in Kansas, I get a call from Tom, who tells me our bear was a two-year-old male. I think about that *was* for a minute. That was quick. "Young males are usually the troublemakers," he says. "But he should be out of your hair now."

I thank him for his help.

Bears continue to wander around Ed and Gwyn's for more than a month, worrying Ross at night and into the early morning. If Tom caught one sibling and the other remains, is the one who remains subdued or even angrier than before? Ed goes to Trinidad to research guns, a sentence I never thought I would write. We're curious about the use of rubber bullets, which seems less violent to us, and possibly a good idea while the bears are unsettled.

But no dice. Apparently, you can get rubber bullets only through law enforcement. Huh. Seems bizarre. Ed shrugs it off as a bad idea.

Whatever. We're in Iowa, where bears are uncommon, especially by our home in the middle of Des Moines. Still, even here, I often awake in the night, hearing some sound or another—the ice-maker dumping cubes or a branch hitting the window in the breeze—and my heart begins its drill, beating faster and faster, thumping in my chest.

Breathe in, breathe out.

You're safe.

Am I?

19. Our Bodies Break

I don't intentionally stalk the psychologist to talk about all this; we meet at a party and he is sitting at a table all by himself, not talking to anyone, so I visit with him about his work. He mentions specializing in PTSD, and bingo, I am off.

According to the National Institutes of Mental Health, PTSD, or post-traumatic stress disorder, stems from a healthy response to danger, the "fight or flight" reaction that is hard-wired into our brains. It only becomes a mental health issue in people who continue to feel frightened a month or longer after the event, when they are not in danger. Symptoms include avoiding the place of danger and being easily startled, feeling on edge, and having trouble sleeping.

It's been four months since the bear's visits and I still have panic attacks at night. And just the thought of going back to the cabin starts the whole clammy-hands, heart-thumping, *Oh-my-God-I-am-a-mess* process.

I sit down at the table across from the psychologist.

"This is probably small potatoes compared to what you deal with," I begin. "But I feel I have a little PTSD after a forest fire at our Colorado cabin last year, and then floods, and a bear that kept trying to break in this year." Then, I add: "I was never really probably in danger."

He looks at me silently for a second.

"First, it is nothing to apologize for," he finally says. "And you only have to *feel* like you are in danger, whether you actually are or not. This is about emotions, not reason. Plus, I think a fire, flood, and bear sounds pretty scary."

I almost cry. Seriously. Why had I never thought of actually talking to a professional about this? I'm a health writer—I've written many pieces about the difference between sadness and depression, about PTSD, about the need to face our feelings. Still, I had tried to deny my emotions. I was OK during the day, so I didn't feel the need for help. This being human thing is hard.

The psychologist says I'd be stunned at the number of people who suffer from PTSD after an accident or the loss of a loved one, home, job, or anything that had made them feel safe. It's not just soldiers and war.

"How do you treat it?" I ask him.

"Journaling," he says. "Writing about it."

Writing, he says, causes patients to mentally revisit the event and may help control their fear. I knew this, of course. I also knew that emotions usually trump reason. That feeling a particular way is not a cause for guilt because I don't choose to feel that way. And, far from wallowing in these feelings, I have been actually denying them, deciding this all was no big deal because I could wallop it with Ambien.

But the whole writing thing really hits me. I wrote as therapy after my cancer diagnosis. I even wrote about writing for therapy. Yet I started this book a year ago and stopped right before the latest flood, which was right before the bear. It has been sitting in my computer, gathering virtual dust.

I thank the psychologist for his good advice and then promptly do not take it. In fact, it is more than a year before I return to writing this book.

Instead of facing my emotions, I start developing a strategy to completely wrap the cabin in electric wire. But, no matter the system, the issue of the doors remains. Electrifying them but keeping them usable is tricky. People remind me that the problem bear is gone.

"He's dead, dead, dead," Gwyn says. Three times dead.

I buy heavy-duty pepper spray. I get it in the mail and do a practice run, as instructed, and am ready for bear. Or not. You have to aim carefully, at the bear's face because it only works if you get his nose. But you have a certain amount of leeway: The spray reaches 75 feet. It is best used after a bear starts to charge.

Imperfect, but it's at least something.

· · ·

I finally start sleeping better and am in the middle of deep and restful slumber when Joe, on the last Friday of August, wakes me up at 4 a.m. "I think I should go to the ER," he says. He's been fighting severe stomach pain for a couple of hours. I throw on my clothes, we jump into the car and, within half an hour, he is in a hospital bed.

Thus begins ten months in which all of us get sick. First Joe, then Ed, Gwyn, and me. Two diagnoses of cancer, one cancer scare, and one rare bile duct disease.

It's difficult not to tie these illnesses to the fire, to consider it perhaps the last straw in our bodies' defense systems. Toxic air plus the physical and mental stress of trying to right the wrongs being done to nature have taken a toll on us.

ER docs find a shadow in Joe's bile duct, but tests are unclear about the cause. Over the next few weeks, he gets an alphabet soup of tests, an MRI, MRCP, and ERCP, all of which examine the liver, gallbladder, bile ducts, pancreas, and pancreatic duct.

Specialists in Des Moines believe he has bile duct cancer, which kills within a year or two. Of course, we don't want to accept that, so we go to the Mayo Clinic in Minnesota, fully expecting them to disagree. Instead, they confirm the diagnosis—this is more than likely terminal cancer.

It's surreal to face Joe's death. My husband, lover, best friend. I can't envision a life without him. A world without him somewhere. So I don't envision it. I've shown aptitude in denial before. I can do it again. This is just not going to happen.

Mayo docs want to do another MRCP on their own machines, which they can read better. This one blessedly, thankfully commutes Joe's death sentence. It's not cancer, but a massive blockage caused by gallstones in the bile duct. Surgeons remove the stones and diagnose him with a rare disease the name of which he can't even remember.

"What's that thing I have?" he asks me.

I have to think a bit, getting the words correct and in proper order. "Primary sclerosing cholangitis," I answer. That means scarring and inflammation of the bile ducts. It's serious business and could cause an infection that would kill him. But it's not terminal cancer.

Docs give him an ongoing prescription of pain pills and antibiotics. As soon as he gets a gut ache, which is a sign of inflammation, he takes the antibiotics to fight the infection and the pain pills to get him through the first few days. He has to have regular procedures to clean out his ducts.

But he will live. He will live. He will live. And once he recovers, he's as active and energetic as ever. I often look at him alongside me as we walk around the lake near our home, and smile. There he is, right there, walking with me. Where he belongs.

Almost all the information I can find on Joe's condition links it to heavy drinking and obesity. Joe likes his daily wine and an occasional martini, but that is hardly heavy. And I outweigh him by 10 pounds, even though I am of average weight.

Much recent research has looked at the effects of the stress of natural disasters on public health, motivated by the 9/11 attacks. Summing it up, the National Institutes of Health tie such stress to increases in multiple diseases, such as heart attacks and cancer. Oddly enough, at least to me, the list also includes cirrhosis of the liver. So why wouldn't fire, flood, bear, and a psycho wife be at least a partial cause of Joe's liver problems?

Joe has always felt things deeply and internalized them, so while I am panting in terror about natural disasters and huge animals run amok, he is quietly going on about his business with a calm exterior. Inside, though, he is churning, worrying, fretting. And I have been so focused on my own issues, I have not considered how he might be managing all this. I brought home my panic attacks, so he no doubt brought his home as well.

I call Ed and Gwyn, elated to share the news that Joe is going to live. I begin explaining the ERCP, a test I had never heard of before.

"I know," Ed says. "I had one."

"Why?" I ask. "When?"

"A couple months ago. We didn't mention it because of all you were going through. I've had stomach problems, basically since the fire."

"And what did it show?" I ask.

"Lots of inflammation, pretty much everywhere. The doctor says it's stress."

I had known his back and hip bothered him—they always do. And I had known he was deeply sad. I didn't know about the stomach problems. When I told him last summer that I had lost my appetite for Mexican food, he mentioned not being able to tolerate it either. I didn't think any more of it. I had been numb after the fire, protectively unfeeling. That has got to stop, I think. But then, I wonder if my protective shell needs to stay in place for a while longer. Maybe I will molt eventually, like a snake, and once again expose myself again to my feelings.

"It's the fire," Ed says simply.

· · ·

Gwyn noticed the black spot on her arm in the summer, but assumed it was just a charcoal sliver. She has no good answer when asked why she thought walking around with a charcoal sliver was ok.

It's melanoma, the deadliest form of skin cancer. We go through several anxious weeks before surgery. One doctor says it has likely already spread, at least to her lymph nodes. A second one disagrees.

Fortunately, the second doctor is right. Her prognosis is excellent. Surgeons successfully remove the entire tumor, which is small, only .9 mm, and it has not spread. It's early stage. Highly survivable.

She also has several cancerous spots on her face that were frozen but have returned. These are likely basal cell, which are far less deadly than melanoma, but still need to be treated with chemo creams. She buys a new hat, stocks up on sunscreen, and religiously applies her chemo.

"I plan to be more careful in the future," she says. Like most cancer patients, she blames herself. But she has been exposed to intense sun on a mountaintop that no longer has shade. And sun exposure is a direct cause of skin cancer.

• • •

In May I go in for a routine mammogram. The radiologist invites me into his lab to look at my film. *This is a first*, I think. *This can't be good.*

He shows me the calcifications in my breast, uneven sizes and shapes, and he makes it clear he thinks I have breast cancer again. Very small, very early. A biopsy confirms his suspicions, and I am again diagnosed with triple-negative breast cancer, a fairly rare type that is not fueled by hormones and does not respond to typical treatment like tamoxifen or Arimidex. This is a second primary cancer, not a recurrence of the cancer I had in 2006. And it is less than half the size of my previous cancer, which I beat, so I can beat this one again. Easily.

Bloody hell, though! I was the upbeat, helpful advocate, blogger, and author after my first diagnosis. Nothing was going to get me down. I cannot repeat that role. In January, I had stopped blogging, telling my readers I'd had my say and I was done with cancer. Apparently, it wasn't done with me.

It's been one nasty blow after another for the past two years. I've always been a one-foot-in-front-of-the-other kind of woman, a problem-solver, the one who sees the light at the end of the tunnel. I now only see a dank, dark tunnel. Maybe I hear a train.

The cancer is in the same breast, so a lumpectomy is not going to work, as those need radiation and I can't be radiated in the same breast twice. A mastectomy is the only real option, as I see it, and if I have to go down that road, I will get both sisters lopped off. I don't want to be a one-breasted wonder.

The surgery goes well, and I recover fine. But I keep thinking: *Why? Why again?*

Stress? Toxic air after the fire, or even during it?

The radiologist mentions that calcifications like mine can be caused by previous radiation. She doesn't say it, but I link the second cancer to the treatment for my first cancer, exacerbated by twice-yearly mammograms and regular x-rays for my emphysema.

But the fire? One thing I have learned in my cancer research is that everything is connected in some way. Adding a new stress or toxin to our biological system will cause something somewhere to go out of whack.

In fact, recent research at the University of Florida directly links increases in air pollution, like that after a forest fire, to breast cancer. Specifically, pollution changes hormone levels and increases breast density, and women with dense breasts have a six-fold increase in the risk of breast cancer.

Plus, there's the stress of dealing with our natural disaster.

So, yes, my cancer was connected to previous treatment but also to toxic air and stress. This fire is just the gift that keeps on giving.

Friends encourage me to head to the mountain, to sit on my deck and soak up the sun, to rest and relax and regain my strength. They have no idea. The mountain is work now. It is no longer the healer. Now, it needs healing itself.

Gwyn has been spraying weeds for the past two months and suggests I can help with that if I don't feel strong enough for other tasks. But after two bouts of cancer, I am staying as far away from chemicals as I can.

She says if the poison in the herbicides kills her, so be it. She will have left a healthier mountain behind.

"Well I, for one, don't want it to kill you," I say.

"Thanks," she says.

And, by the way, I don't want it to kill me either.

We're not yet fully licensed to navigate this new life in which so much is not as it should be or as it has been, when everything seems sideways, knocked off its base. Our compass is cloudy at best, completely broken at worst. Our mental paths, if mapped, would look like doodles created by a two-year-old with new crayons—circles, jagged lines, stops and starts in black, green, orange, blue.

As I write this book, it becomes clear why I have been avoiding it. I'd not yet put all the losses and stresses and pain together. Now that I do, I am dazed and grateful that I didn't try to process it earlier.

I wonder if it even makes sense for us to go to the mountain this year, that I might actually heal better in Iowa. Do yoga in the park, eat farmer's market veggies, walk around the lake and down to the river.

But I can't not go. Mother Mountain is sitting by the phone, waiting for me to call. I need to be there. Whether it's the best place to heal or not, we're going.

PART THREE

Climate Grief

20. Yellow Fingernails

Most of the pirate's eye and nose are gone, his beard a pale shadow, barely visible against the rock of the mountain. His eye patch, plume, and part of his hat are mostly alive, the rest is burned away. Huge gaunt tendrils of burned trees reach toward the peak, sallow and lifeless, nothing growing for acres. Then, some spots of greenish fuzz, probably weeds sprouting in the dead earth. And, occasionally, a grove of evergreens, wondrously alive.

By contrast, our ridge is barely recognizable. The locust trees have overtaken way too much, their hard, thorny arms blocking our way past them. But we have aspen groves with some trees taller than us. Acres of grassy meadows surround the carcasses of dead pines and firs. And weeds with leaves the size of tennis rackets lurk demonically, evil opportunists sprouting wherever they can.

Ed has plowed five-foot-wide grass paths through it all, like something Miss Marple would walk on. Our old paths are completely gone, run over by a rampage of greenery here, by weeds and felled trees elsewhere.

In the burn area, not a single evergreen has sprouted naturally. The only live trees are those we planted. It's clear the fire destroyed the seeds the forest needs to propagate itself.

Most of the grass is from seed Gwyn spread. Some is from the areas I seeded. The rest is natural growth nourished by heavy snow over the winter. Happily, there must be enough vegetation of some sort higher upstream to stem erosion, as there have been only minor floods on the creek this year, nothing to threaten the garden or the cabin.

It's June 2015, two years after the fire.

Ed and Gwyn have a new greenhouse, three times the size of their old one, settled on higher ground, way above the creek, with corn, tomatoes, peppers, and squash. The garden remains behind its wall next to the creek and is a burst of health popping from the soil. Gwyn's own Whole Foods produce section. We get here too late to enjoy the best of it, but we still have several fresh salads and veggie dishes straight from the earth.

We can only find a few dozen of the seedlings we planted last year and those look healthy, but most of their cousins are trapped under thick batches of locusts. Had we been here earlier in the summer, we could have cut the shrubs and opened the baby trees to the light, but if we try it now, we risk killing our seedlings. We can only hope the trees are alive and well down in the thorns and leaves somewhere.

The weather is warm, but not too hot, with cool, pleasant nights. Often, though, a smoky haze settles over the mountain, residue of forest fires in Washington and Oregon. We compulsively check online reports to make sure the fires are there and not here, but wish they were nowhere.

I take a photo of a hawk in a nearby tree. It's a great shot, close enough to see him in his regal haughtiness and I smile at his return to the forest. The photo itself makes me cringe, though, because all I can see in the background are tons of dead trees on the mountain. Not a hint of life beyond the hawk.

The fire damage on the peak itself is even more obvious this year. It's all on the northwest side of the mountain, with a clear delineation right under the peak; to the northeast, the forests are as they had been—giant stands of pines, fir, spruce, aspens. To the northwest, only sparse patches of evergreens grow, with no visible aspens. The valleys on the peak continue to deepen, boulders keep shifting, building deepener ruts.

The cabin looks at us meekly when we first drive up, covered in the boards Joe had nailed on last year, like a bit of a beggar in the meadow. It seems to say: *What have I ever done to you to make you treat me like this?*

• • •

Ed has taken the boards off the side door so he could get in to hook up our gas, water, and solar, as he sweetly does every year, but the rest of the cherry red barriers remain.

"Do you want me to take them down?" Joe asks.

"Let's leave them for a few days," I say. They rob the cabin of light, but the boards are a safety shield should a bear come by again; they help me ease into the whole business of being here.

Ed and Gwyn have seen only a couple of bears so far, and those have been on the other side of the creek, far enough from us to be completely non-threatening. Many have no doubt moved to better grazing areas after the fire, and those who remain have more vegetation to eat this year, with a decent amount of shrubs, grass, and berries.

Ed has fixed our bathroom screen and is in the midst of fixing our front screen door, which the bear left in a twisted mess we thought couldn't be repaired. We hadn't counted on Ed's ability to fix whatever.

It takes us longer than usual to clean the cabin because we have an extra thick coating of flies. We think it's because we were so late in getting here. Or maybe the cabin being darker encouraged more insects. Some even got into the wicker basket we use for blanket storage and into our cedar cabinet. The black gunk looks like mouse poop, but there are no signs of mice anywhere—nothing is chewed or torn. I throw away a couple of blankets and some shirts and pants that are stained with the stuff.

"We could take them to town and wash them," Joe objects.

"Ewww," I answer. They look toxic to me, so they go into the trash. They were pretty ratty to begin with. Later, we discover a hole in the attic through which bats got into the cabin. We mend it quickly, but I realize that what I thought was mouse poop could have been bat guano, not only nasty, but potentially dangerous as it can lead to histoplasmosis. A fresh new lung disease I'd never thought of.

Over the winter, Joe made some unwelcome mats to put by the windows closest to the bedroom to keep bears away. They have screws with the sharp side pointing up, in a grid two inches apart in each direction. The sharp edges would pinch a bear's paw, but the wide placement protects from serious injury. I don't entirely trust them—I figure a bear could just push the mat aside if he was really motivated. But the forest service recommends them; they would at least slow the beast down and give us good warning.

I fill the bathroom with unscented soaps, lotions, and shampoos I got at the farmer's market in Des Moines. We put fresh spices in the rack on the kitchen wall but shut the nearby window at night so the smells don't intrigue a passing bear.

In two days, I agree to let Joe take all the boards down. I still get tense when we shut the lights off, but now it's more of an overall tension, a quiet shaking. Less a panic attack and more a lingering stress. I still wear my earplugs and take Ambien.

I keep the bear spray on the chest near the bed, next to the car alarm, ready for action because the darkness still feels dangerous. The last flood whooshed through while I slept, the bear tried to break in during the night, Joe's need to rush to the ER even happened in the dark. So why should I trust the night? I think of the first time the bear came, and how Joe and I went back to sleep for two hours afterwards, feeling safe because the sun was up by then. We had light.

I mention this to a friend who is an Episcopal priest. "We're all afraid of the dark," she says, simply. It's true. But when that darkness actually brings danger, these inbred fears are legitimized. There really is a monster under the bed.

My best sleep comes in the safety of the early morning, after the sun has risen, so sometimes I am barely awake by the time Ed visits on his way to work in the forest. I try to disguise my laxness, try to act like I have been up for hours, as he has, feeling guilty that I am not already out battling weeds. Then I remember I have my own battles and only energy enough to fight a few of those.

I want to just give in and be a grump. Just be honest about it. OK, I often am a grump. And Joe is no Mr. Sunshine. He's still on edge, waiting for his gut to revolt. And he's still tired from surgery and from stress over just about everything.

I have more pain and discomfort than I expected from surgery, and I try to take it easy, but the weeds are gargantuan, new residents of our paradise, who come with bad habits and obviously know nothing about birth control. Any soil that had been disturbed by the burn or by fire trucks or loggers now sprouts legions of thistle and mullein. Sections of our back ridge are like some alien planet, growing these green beasts, many taller than me, that have to be hacked down with a saw. And they grow in groves, insidious creatures that hide behind bushes, looking innocent and green when they are actually plotting to take over the world.

As with most plants, these have a certain beauty: thistle flowers are a lustrous purple and mullein have stately yellow stalks and velvety sage green leaves.

Gwyn has been spraying them with increasingly strong herbicide. But they are insistent on making this land their land.

Many areas that, like the Rockies, are facing climate change are also battling invasive species. Even the Galapagos Islands, where Darwin perfected his theory of the origins of species, are threatened. In fact, a 2007 UNESCO report lists species such as invasive blackberries and red quinine trees as one of the greatest threats to the islands. They're pushing out the natural orchids.

My contribution to our invasion is to take the heads off the blooming thistle. I hike up to the ridge, putting my iPhone on speaker and blasting the Everly Brothers across the acres, letting any nearby bears know I am coming, armed with vintage harmonies.

Somewhere, off in the woods, a giant furry creature is humming, *Wake Up, Little Susie.*

I carry a 30-gallon plastic garbage sack tucked into my belt on the left hip and bear spray in a carrying case on the right hip. I clip the thistle heads, sometimes having to reach up a foot or two to grab them. Smaller plants have up to 15 buds and bigger ones have 20 or more, so I fill the sack without moving more than a few feet. The plastic proves an ill-conceived idea, as the thistles break through and scratch my legs as I walk. I take the bag off my hip and rest it on my walking stick to give the abrasive thorns their distance.

Finally, I decide to do what my friends instructed: Sit on my deck, relax, and heal. I read, take photos, do some sketches, and take small walks.

I think I become less of a grump, but you might ask others to verify that.

•   •   •

A yellow ball glows at the far end of the meadow, on the Bear Highway.

It begins to move, morphs into an oval, then stretches out into the shape of a bear cub. A little blond guy, with sun sparkling off his fur, so he looks like he's plugged into a socket. When his rear end faces me, it's round and shiny, like a little planet that just landed in the meadow. I whisper to Joe to come see it. He's been cleaning off his clippers, ready to cut weeds, and comes to stand next to me on the deck. We see a second cub and, in the pines behind them, mama. Mama and the other cub are both brown, so the blond guy is the golden boy, or girl, of the family.

The baby bears are rooting in the grass under the scrub oak, probably eating the acorns that have fallen there. We watch the cubs, and mama watches us. She doesn't budge but stands as a silent sentry over her kids. They stay there for about half an hour, the cubs grazing contentedly, then slowly move up the hill onto Dominic's road, away from us and into the trees. Mama takes one last look at us before she disappears in the trees.

That's as close to bears as we get this summer, so maybe they got the word.

Ed putts up later on Alice, on his way back from helping Gwyn spray the weeds. We tell him about the bears. He's not seen the little family yet, but it's clear there is enough food for the bears to stay away from us. And I hope mama can stay with both cubs until they're settled in the world and know how to fend for themselves.

I sit in our porch swing; Ed and Joe are both on Adirondack chairs. One chair is a beautiful oak thing Joe made. The other is a piece of plastic from Safeway. The swing is canvas and came from a garage sale in Des Moines. We'll never make *Architectural Digest* up here.

I look out toward the Bear Highway to the stand of 50-foot evergreens that jut from the earth, soldier-straight. They climb halfway up the hill and extend from our land. Mountain beauties, reminders of how it used to be, blessed survivors of the fire.

"Those trees are amazing," I say.

"Yeah," Ed says. "Thanks to me and Joe."

"Those?" I ask, pointing across the meadow.

"Those," he says. "We put out fires there."

"Yes, we did," Joe agrees.

We have often talked about what Ed and Joe did up here in the fire's pause between the first and second burns, with their hoses and buckets and rags. But I have always thought they worked just between our places, not far over there, across the meadow. I hadn't even considered how some of the greenery I gaze at every morning exists because of them.

"Whoa," I say. "Thanks. And good job!"

Ed chuckles, proud of himself, happy with that bit of success.

"It's good," he says.

And we quietly gaze appreciatively at our massive green neighbors.

I think about the psychologist who told me to write about my experience with the bear. Face it, he said.

I should return to writing this book, my little guilty alter ego says, but I get no farther than a few notes about how things look now and what we're doing this year. Scattered jots on my computer and in my notebook. Random, bursts about bumblebees stuck in the window screens and the color of the mountain. Shades of grey.

It makes all the sense in the world to face my fears by writing about them, but to be fair, I am up here actually facing the reality. And as the days pass, I feel my nighttime stress lightening more and more, but not yet disappearing.

I'm not yet ready to go quietly into any night.

• • •

Gwyn's fingernails are yellow from the poison she is spraying onto the plants. It's almost a daily ritual for her, broken only on washdays and, occasionally, when she admits she is exhausted.

She lost more than 30 pounds from her exercise regimen this winter and she's lithe, even sinewy, almost the size she was when I first met her when she and Ed got married 46 years ago, but much more muscular, much stronger in all ways. I remember her then, petite and pretty, always well-groomed and more feminine than I. Which is to say, feminine. At that time, I would have laughed out loud at this 67-year-old Gwyn who has her own well-used chainsaw and ATV.

Those many decades ago, she deferred to Ed's stronger personality. Now she defers to nobody. Still, I wish she would listen to our concerns about her exposure to chemicals. She just had melanoma surgery and she is still fighting the basal cancer spots on her face. She remains adamant, though, that she is killing those weeds, even if they kill her.

We're having dinner at Ed and Gwyn's with Russ, who is here for a long weekend. He mentions the fingers.

"Killing these weeds will be my legacy," she says again. "If they kill me, it will be for a good cause." Ed's face is pained. We're all silent.

"What about living to 100?" I ask. She and Joe both have this as a goal, one I do not share.

"Maybe I'm building up resistance and I'll live forever," she says.

Russ sort of groans, Ed sighs, Joe mutters.

She started spraying with 2,4 D, an herbicide that's been linked to cancers such a non-Hodgkin's lymphoma—blood cancer—and soft-tissue sarcoma and to reproductive problems, according to the Natural Resources Defense Council, which has sued the Environmental Protection Agency because of its failure to ban it. It works by changing the way cells in the plants grow. Still, it is widely used in popular suburban lawn products, especially "weed and feed" combos that mix fertilizers with herbicides. The label warns that, if it gets on you, rinse the skin immediately with plenty of water for 15-20 minutes and call a poison control center or doctor for treatment advice. Gwyn says she rinses her hands thoroughly and that the yellow on her fingertips is just a stain, not the poison itself. I think any product that tells you to wash yourself for 20 minutes and then to call the poison control center is bad stuff.

And the 2,4 D doesn't even work. She moves on to Milestone, which is recommended by the Colorado State Extension service to control early growth mullein, at the floret stage.

It has low toxicity to humans but can irritate the respiratory system and even cause lung damage to some people, according to its Materials Safety Data Sheet. It is effective in much lower doses than other herbicides, making it an improvement, but there's no guarantee against residual effects on plants and animals or long-term damages to humans. Gwyn uses a mask and gloves and avoids working on windy days. And, ironically, what she applies is probably less than the amount of toxins used in our neighborhood in Des Moines. But that's like choosing between cutting off your left finger or your right hand. Neither should be a goal. I continue to be uneasy because of Gwyn's health and because of the extra toxins that are now in the ground and the air.

Milestone works only on the smallest mullein, which is tricky because the stuff can honestly grow a foot overnight. Once, on a walk, Joe broke a stalk of mullein in half. Two days later, there were three new shoots coming from the break. We measured the longest: 13 inches. In two days.

When mullein gets that big, the only thing you can do is break it in pieces and twist the break line to disrupt and discourage new shoots. It doesn't kill easily, and you want to get it before it flowers, as one flower can have 100,000 seeds, which can live in the ground as long as 100 years. If you can catch it when it is small enough and the ground has some give to it, you can pull it out by its roots.

I try spraying mullein with undiluted vinegar, and it does nothing. The plants remain their normal sage green and continue to grow like something in a 1950s film about nuclear effects. Joe tries a mixture of vinegar and salt with the same effect. We end up pulling, cutting, or mangling larger plants. At this time of year, we have few small plants, but when we find those, we pull them out.

That's painful to our hands and backs and is seriously slow going, with weeds popping up behind us almost as soon as we pull others out. Gwyn's approach is far more efficient and effective.

We are faced with bad choices.

21. Resurrection

A spider crawls across my face in the middle of the night. I swat it, then fall right back to sleep. I momentarily think about there being a bat in here again, but don't dwell on it. I just go back to sleep, assuming it wasn't a brown recluse. Probably a harmless and helpful daddy longlegs.

No panic.

I wake as the sun is just rising, put on my purple chenille robe, make a hot cup of tea, wrap myself in an afghan and go to the deck to watch the sun come up. The thermometer reads 51 degrees; it will jump quickly with the warmth of the sun, but today should be a reasonable one, in the 70s at most.

We have one hummingbird feeder out—we hope it's high enough to not appeal to a bear—and the little guys are just showing up, zipping from the willows by the creek to the feeder and back, getting their morning juice. The mountain is all in blue shadows, tucked in an early morning mist; the sun reflects golden sparks off rock outcroppings on the peak.

Sunflowers are plentiful this year—Gwyn had planted some on the ridge last year, trying to push out the weeds, and a few of the seeds made their way to the cabin. We have three stalks growing behind the rock in front of our deck, more than eight feet tall. Behind that, the sky is all yellows and oranges, a celebration of a new day. It would take conscious work to feel hopeless in the sight of all this.

I breathe air so brisk and clean it feels like its own anti-toxin, watching miracles abound—the sunrise, the mountain, the hummingbirds. I inhale deeply and smile.

Far away, I hear the calls of elks. At first, I think it's cows; moms can yell this loud when a baby is out of sight. But we have no cows this year, so I listen more closely. Yep, that's the bugling of elk. Then, quiet. They have moved on.

I hear Joe puttering about inside. Now that he's awake I turn on the radio to listen to NPR's Morning Edition and open the side window so I can hear it on the deck. Time to learn what has happened in the world in the past few hours. What a way to lose a good mood. I shut it off.

Joe joins me with his banana and tea. I sit in the swing, facing the mountain and he is in a chair facing the meadow.

We have a new family of eagles on the far ridge and the fledglings glide over and along the meadow, their screeches announcing their arrival, like kids on a playground. They light in one tree, then another, one bird leading the way, and two others following from here to there, and there, and there.

This is resurrection, these new lives flying in front of us. This is hope. The sun, the hummingbirds, the elk, the fledglings. All of it. All of blessed it. We've seen a couple Steller's Jays and at least one Western Tanager, so some of our other colorful birds might also be returning.

When we first moved here, birds were so plentiful that we'd sit on the deck with my bird book, trying to identify all the different types: the tanagers and jays bright orange and blue against the lush green, plus chickadees, buntings, meadowlarks, warblers, and robins. As the years got hotter and drier, we saw fewer and fewer, so even before the fire it was unusual to see more than two or three different birds in a day. The heat and the loss of vegetation to drought and disease turned this once welcoming place into a dead zone. Again, it's part of a worldwide pattern—the earth has lost nearly 30 percent of its birds since 1970.

I wonder how long we could just lounge on our deck, just breathing it all in. Just breathing. We eat our cereal and blueberries in the open air, lazy buggers up to nothing here on our mountain.

Ross comes bounding up to the deck and stops for a minute to say hello and be petted. Bella runs by, as always unimpressed with our existence. Both rush down to the creek and splash, then return to the deck to share the mud with us. Soon Ed drives up on Alice, kills the engine at the culvert, then pulls his legs over and comes up the path.

"What are you two up to today?" he asks.

"So far, nothing," I answer.

"And I could do that the rest of the day," Joe adds.

Joe says he plans to cut down a few more dead trees. I say I have some writing to do, which I always do. Writers can always write, whether or not anybody ever reads it. Maybe I will return to this book.

I mention the elk. Ed had seen them in the upper meadow. A small herd, maybe only 10 or so. But healthy and active citizens of the forest. More than we had before the fire, when it was too dry here for them.

The bears are behaving, and the rest of the animals are returning, although fewer in number. Life is swelling in the woods; the elk are lured by the grass, the eagles have found enough live trees remaining, and the hummingbirds are good as long as we keep them sugared up.

"Progress," I say.

"Progress," Ed agrees. "But now to work." He drives across the meadow to a burned grove of aspens, and soon we hear the sound of his saw.

Joe puts on his work clothes, grabs his chain saw and goes the other way, up the ridge, to do the same thing. Soon, I hear the whine of his saw. Then quiet. I used to worry when the silences were too long, imagining Joe crushed under a tree. Once I went to check up on him and he was just sitting under an aspen, staring calmly into space, sipping his water, his chain saw about ten feet away, next to some freshly cut logs.

Now, I realize the spaces between buzzes increase as the years go by, but I still listen for the eventual sounds that assure me he's safe.

I retreat to the inside of the cabin, to a space that feels manageable to me. I begin to clean out the oak bachelor's closet Joe made, a handsome piece of furniture, with recessed panels and molding on top and bottom. It's only four feet wide, so we can't have too many clothes here.

I start throwing away jeans that are just too ugly to wear anymore, torn shirts, and uncomfortable shoes. I tear some up for rags and fold the good things to give to the shelter in town.

I look at a chair we bought used last year that has a broken spring; I think about replacing it, but the process of disposal and delivery are just too cumbersome to be worth it. We hang on to things way beyond their use-by date because when we're tired of something, we can't just throw it in the garbage or take it to the curb, tag it, and expect the city to pick it up. We have to take care of it ourselves, including lugging it out of the cabin, into Mr. Green Jeans, and down the mountain.

But we've needed a new shed for our batteries ever since we built the cabin, so I stop cleaning and get online. I use my iPhone, which has a signal so slow it feels like it's crawling up the mountain on meandering goats. Our existing shed is big enough for the two enormous batteries we use for our solar power, plus our generator. Ed made it when we first built the cabin, hammering it together in about an hour, but it's plywood that's weathered badly. It's never been mice-proof.

When Joe gets back, we finally select a shed and order it online. A week later, we meet the delivery truck on the county road— Neither UPS nor FedEx will deliver all the way up here —and bring up a box the size of a dining room table. It takes Joe two days to assemble because he doesn't have the right tools, the right ground, or the right energy. Once it's finished, though, it's as though the storage gods have shined on us. So much extra room, we're not even sure how to use it.

It's heartening to have this new structure, even if it is only a prefab shed. It's a sign of progress of sorts, a sign we're reaffirming our roots here. A sign we can actually get something done.

Our healthy seedlings, the vibrant grass, the elk and eaglets, all point toward the rebirth we have so dearly dreamed of. Not biblical-level resurrection, just incremental steps, mostly leading forward.

22. Burn Scars

The oaks and aspens are starting to change color and the nights are cool enough for blankets; in the mornings we often need a fire. Sometimes we take a fattening but aromatic short cut and heat the cabin by baking cinnamon rolls. Gwyn's garden has a bumper crop of squash; some juicy tomatoes hang from dried-up vines, but for the most part, it is time to prepare the soil for next year.

Snow falls on the mountain but melts the next day. It's nearly 7 a.m. before the sun is up, and it sets by 7:30 p.m. Both days and nights are cool, and I now can sometimes sleep without Ambien. The bear spray and car alarm remain on the chest next to the bed, the unwelcome mats are under the windows, and the doors are locked.

I still put my iPhone music on high volume when I walk alone, and I still carry my bear spray in its handy sling on my hip.

We've not been that social this year. We've visited Harlan and Pat a couple of times but haven't seen Pearl. I call Melva to check in and see about stopping by, but Pearl is now in a nursing home in Pueblo.

We finally invite Dave for dinner. It's the first time we've seen him since the year of the fire. He comes in the back way, driving through his meadow, parking his truck at the end of the road, a few hundred feet away from Ed and Gwyn's outhouse, and walking from there. He takes off his handgun and holster and leaves them on Gwyn's horse trailer.

He and his siblings have been trying to keep up with miles of fence repairs and acres of logging and are pondering what and how to plant to keep the weeds down and control erosion. He and Gwyn talk weeds and spray and other processes.

I want to share funny stories about his growing up on this mountain, about our neighbors when they were young, as we used to.

But not tonight. Levity is not invited.

Still, it is good to see Dave, good to see all our neighbors, all the people who comprise our rural community, who share our collective trauma. But when we meet, we cannot get beyond the fire and its scars. It's our social cement right now, eclipsing the chats we once had about grandkids and books and recipes. We wear our scars defiantly, ready to fight, to face the next upheaval, whatever that might be, but we're not the people we had been.

We leave a few days earlier than planned because I have a seroma—a buildup of fluid near my breast surgery site. I've had several of these after my mastectomy, and the surgeon drains them with a needle the size of a Volkswagen. They're not life-threatening, nor a sign of a problem, but they are uncomfortable. This one is a doozy and looks like a bruise. It ends up being an ecchymosis, a large area of subcutaneous bleeding. Not a long-term problem, just another medical oddity in this, the year that our bodies revolted.

At the very least, we're all tired. Even Ed and Gwyn plan to leave within the week, more than a month earlier than usual.

As usual, I visit Mom and Dad's graves before I leave, talking to them, listening to the answers I know they'd give:

You'll be fine. The trees you planted look good. Just keep at it. It will get better. That's Mom, always the one to encourage me, to tell me I am up to whatever challenge.

You need to get here early next year and cut down the locusts so your trees can make it. And keep cutting that dead wood so it doesn't fall on you. That's Dad, the taskmaster, telling me to get with the ticket, and stay with it.

I feel grounded to this Earth, this ground and this planet, but I can envision an eagle's view of my tiny self, standing next to the graves in the aspen grove, with a lush green meadow in front of me and a gnarly road behind, leading down the mountain, past Harlan and Pat's, past Pearl's, to the county road, and to town.

I am so very small. I imagine flying higher to see the roof of the cabin on the road in the other direction, then Ed and Gwyn's little spread, then higher up to see the scout camp where the fire started, still higher to see houses on Bear Creek, including Dave's, with its little pond. I can see the burn scars on the ridge behind me and the ridge in front of me, continuing up to the peak.

Higher up, and the landscape turns to green on both sides, past the burn scars. To areas untouched by the fire. In all this loss, the promise of the land remains, the assurance of this colossal organism that lives and breathes and moves. I am a microscopic atom in it all, a miniscule particle that really is not needed here, trying hard to be productive, helpful, a good little citizen atom.

I used to leave the land with tears in my eyes, saying goodbye to my favorite place on earth. Now, I leave in frustration and exhaustion, wondering what will greet us next year.

• • •

In February, I get an email from Gwyn telling me that 85 mph winds are forecast on our land. She and Ed plan to go there the next day to check things out. For a point of comparison: Hurricanes blow at least 74 mph and moderate tornadoes are between 73 and 112 mph. So 85 mph winds are major. With a forest of dead trees in its path, this storm could be a doozy. I watch my email for Gwyn's note and am about to call when I get her update:

"Well, the houses are OK. The magnitude of the wind damage to the already dead and some live trees is still hard for us to take in. I don't think we've been so overwhelmed since the fire. Some whole trees are down, but most of the mess is from the tops of the trees that blew off. There is hardly a place to walk. It's not like we didn't expect the trees to fall down, but I guess we were hoping for them to fall down one at a time over the next 20 years."

I also had expected the trees to be orderly and fall down one or two at a time so we could keep up with them. Naiveté attacks again. You'd think we'd get a clue about all this by now, but we're just still hoping the worst is behind us. Nevertheless, this will be the year of the wind and falling green trees.

"Your battery shed was blown apart, but Ed fixed it," she adds. "My greenhouse had a panel blown off, so I need to see how much a new one will be. Sure hope this is it for this winter."

I call and ask about damage to our seedlings. Ed and Gwyn weren't able to get that far in—too many trees in their path—so we'll just hope for now that they weren't smashed in the storm.

"We're planning to clear up the trails and leave the rest alone," Ed says. "We can only do what we can do." I thank him for fixing our shed, and he tells me it now has some sort of issue with the doors shutting correctly—it apparently wasn't built to stand up to a mini-tornado. The little improvement we made last year, that gave us a sense of progress, is now another project to fix.

I ask Ed about his stomach pains, which seem to be better, or at least he says they are. Like Joe, he has been taking probiotics and both of them have been enjoying sauerkraut, a natural probiotic as long as it is fermented and not made with vinegar. Ed, always ready to make everything himself, found a small sauerkraut kit that works in a Mason jar. I buy one for Joe for his birthday.

Weather permitting, they'll move to the mountain for the summer in April. We'll go in June. I ordered aspen trees and potentilla bushes from the Forest Service to plant around the cabin, to keep our homestead cheery. I have begun thinking small. I can perhaps control the few acres we can see from our deck, especially given that most of it did not burn.

But clearly, I have been depressed, my second cancer being what finally got to me. The first time I got cancer, I had just lost 50 pounds through diet and exercise. Afterward, I made sure I followed a cancer-fighting diet, including eating the minimum of five servings of vegetables a day and reducing my alcohol intake. (My weakness was enchiladas with green chili, but a person cannot give up everything.) Right before the second cancer, I had lost 10 of the pounds I had regained, again through diet and exercise. So why bother, if my reward for healthy living is cancer?

"Well, you're not dead," Gwyn says brightly. "Something must have worked." I remember my advice to the many women who have written me about breast cancer: All anybody has is today, so live it well. None of us has any guarantee; stewing about problems just ruins your chances of living the life you have. I should listen to my advice.

I ask Gwyn about the cancer on her face. She says it's hard to tell if the cream is working.

"My face looks like pizza," she says. I know nothing about chemo creams and I once would have hit my computer and researched the heck out of it. Now I think I know enough, and I pray for the best.

I have never been a "Why me, Lord?" kind of person, but I do think for now I have had quite enough. But then I look at people who have PTSD that is not likely to go away: soldiers, victims of rape and domestic abuse, survivors of horrific accidents. Or those who live in physical or mental pain. And those who will not outlive their cancer. My problems are small stuff in comparison. We're still standing, and a few acres of our trees are standing with us, green and gorgeous. It's all in your perspective. I am, after all, not dead.

23. Shade We'll Never Sit In

I am talking about our cabin with a friend, and she asks if we're just going to buy land somewhere else, some place without all these problems. Just give up on what we have, leave it behind, and move to a new, green, unspoiled spot. I get this sense of nonchalance from more people than I would like. Few understand what we have lost. Many tease me about my altercation with the bear. I'm fine, so it's funny, right? And most assume that the fire is history and that we have just moved on.

"No," I answer my friend. "This is our land; we want to help it return, if we can." This is not real estate to us; it's not just something we own. It's a part of us. We can't just replace it with something brighter and shinier. It owns us more than we own it.

Like many reasonably affluent Americans, this friend finds joy in shopping, in consuming. When she needs a boost, she buys new clothes or a new piece of furniture. I get this—I love my shoes and rugs and coats and have way too many of them. But the longer I spend on the land, the less I want these things, the lower the value of buying, the higher the value of being.

This mindset has begun to affect my life in Iowa. Living off the grid is an antidote to our disposable culture. I am less interested in stuff. I need less of it.

I think about getting a new area rug for our living room, shop for one online, consider going to an actual store, then decide there's nothing wrong with the old one. I see some cool jeans in a catalog, ponder them, consider size and color, then realize I have enough jeans and throw the catalog away. I find some shoes and order them right away. I didn't say I was perfect.

Our house in Iowa is very much our home—we had it built from a house plan I found in a magazine. It's a *Better Homes and Gardens* Idea Home and it is, honestly, beautiful. We are comfortable here and extremely thankful for our good fortune in having it. But my feelings for this house are different from my connection to the Colorado land. If the house burned, I would be brokenhearted and traumatized. But I could rebuild it, perhaps even better than new. It's manmade, so we can get more men—and women—to make it again. We can't rebuild the land. It's a divine creation and we can only do what we can to help. We didn't make it and we have limited power to remake it.

"Plus," I tell my friend, appealing to her practicality. "We couldn't sell it. It's probably worth half what it was worth before the fire. Who would want to buy acres of burned trees?"

"Well, I suppose that's true," she agrees.

There's a Greek proverb: "A society grows great when old men plant trees whose shade they know they shall never sit in." We are planting the trees because it's simply what needs to be done, as is killing weeds and cutting down dead trees and cleaning up after a flood or wind or all the rest of it. The land needs all this, and we're the ones to do it. We get plenty in return. For more than two decades, this land nourished us, now we need to nourish it. We've been fed; now we feed.

President Franklin D. Roosevelt called forests the "lungs of our land, purifying the air and giving fresh strength to our people." Forests absorb potentially dangerous carbon dioxide while producing healthy oxygen. They trap dust, ash, pollen, and smoke, keeping them out of the air and our lungs. According to American Forests, a single tree can produce enough oxygen in one year to support two people, while absorbing 48 pounds of carbon dioxide and trapping ground-level ozone, carbon monoxide, sulfur dioxide, and other greenhouse gases. In this fire alone, we lost 13,000 acres that had been a natural air filtration plant. The locust bushes and scrub oaks and even the aspens that are growing are no replacement for the towering evergreens we lost.

My burned forest might lead to my friend's lack of good air.

I wish I had thought of that when we were talking, but so much has changed I can't express it with any clarity in a simple conversation. I worry about what faces us at the mountain this year. With so many fallen and falling trees, where is it safe to walk? A guy I used to date was killed by a tree he was cutting on his parents' land, and that has stayed with me for the intervening 50-plus years. When Joe and I were walking in a park in Ljubljana, Slovenia, once, we heard a creaking noise and a huge tree fell in a heavy thud right behind us. Trees can fall randomly. They can kill.

In the past, as I hiked in our Colorado forests, I used to think, "I am so blessed to be here."

Now I look around for what could kill me. Then I slap myself and remind myself I am still blessed to be here. But it could kill me.

I feel that our lives before the fire were a little bit of a fairy tale, grandma and grandpa happily in their little cottage in the woods. But then the darkness came—the fire, floods, the hungry bear, the weeds—and it feels evil and wicked. I remember our lost beauty through a haze of sadness. I don't have the trust I once did that this little corner of paradise will remain untouched by disaster. I work mighty hard to see light and not dark, but I cannot shake the whole, "What's next?"

I stew about my friend's attitude for the rest of the day, and this motivates me even more to finish this book, to tell the story so others understand what this loss means. That the destruction caused by a fire doesn't end at the fire, but continues for years, that it damages the land in immeasurable ways, plus destroys and disrupts animals and humans in its wake, that the aftereffects include more toxins in the air, more threat of extreme weather, more danger to people far beyond our valley.

Writing has helped me honor this land, to recreate what was and what is. As I write about the fire and the floods and the bear, I feel stronger for it. I still jump in the middle of the night when I hear even a slight rustle. When an owl catches some creature and I hear the screeching and animal wailing, I get up, look out into the night, and wonder at the danger of nature. But I go back to sleep, usually without a panic attack.

I have morphed into a significantly different creature in the four years I've been writing this book. My initial focus was on resilience—on how the forest would adapt, and how I would be strong and courageous alongside it. I didn't expect to feel so broken and fearful, so weak.

But I have earned my fear and I no longer deny it nor apologize for it. I am a different kind of strong woman than I envisioned myself to be—I am finally courageous enough to acknowledge my terror.

This began as a memoir about losing our forest to a natural disaster, part of a centuries-old pattern. But the important story here is about our warming planet and dying forests and the enormous increase in the size of forest fires and how much of this is caused by humans and how all of it is exacerbated by our acts— our fire was a natural and unnatural mix, part of a new, more toxic pattern. This isn't just my story. It's the story of a rapidly warming and dangerous world.

It took me six years of writing to finally realize I've been writing a book about grief. I've been grieving the land since day one of the fire, but that sounds way too melodramatic and selfish, plus I have a preternatural need to be above the fray, to be a Zen-like Wonder Woman. Well, to quote my dad, "To hell with that!" I'm in grief, I'm terrified, and the more I engage with people in person and on social media about climate grief, the more I realize I have good company throughout the world. It would, in fact, be inhuman for me—for anybody—to have faced these losses and threats without grieving.

This is more than 35 acres of mountain land to me. It is my parents' legacy and my own. Planting trees is one way to tend this wounded forest; severely reducing our consumption of anything that requires fossil fuels is my personal step toward helping tend a wounded world. But perhaps my real legacy now needs to be educating others about the climate crisis. I worried in the past about being a climate nag. Now I think being silent is immoral.

Writing is my therapy, just as the doctor recommended when I talked with him about my PTSD. This book has been an unexpected exercise in self-discovery. It's taken me about 2,476 rewrites to be open about my emotions, but if this writing is to serve any purpose for me, for you, for anybody, I have to lay it all out there. I'm just going to have to get comfortable being uncomfortable.

I consider adding a map to the book, so I begin drawing our road, the creek, Ed and Gwyn's ranch, the Bryants' house, the dike, and the various trails. It occurs to me that Google Earth would be an asset here, so I find our cabin as seen from the air and am astonished at the accuracy of my little hand-drawn map.

But why should I be surprised? I have walked all these trails for decades and loved every minute and every mile of it, noting milestones and documenting it all in hundreds of photos.

The Google Earth photos must have been taken right after the fire because the ridges are charcoal, with no signs of the greenery that came the next year. Burned trees lie in blackened lines as though giants had been playing pick-up-sticks here. Green trees and grass grow along the road, in the meadow and around the cabin and Ed and Gwyn's buildings, thanks to the firefighters, local volunteers, and Harlan for showing them up here, and for Ed and Joe for coming up in the middle of the fire to help. The meadow is cut in a precise maze of increasingly smaller squares, where Ed had just harvested the hay in his meticulous engineer way.

Ed loves and tends his little ranch, however broken he or it might be, living at least part of his boyhood dream. I always teetered between being a writer and an artist; I made my living writing and teaching and now have returned to painting.

Gwyn also turned to painting, doing one oil of her favorite tree, the perfect fir in Schultz Canyon. It's a gorgeous tree and a gorgeous painting, her rendering of the mountain spectacular. We don't yet know if the tree made it through the most recent windstorm, the latest assault on its life.

Joe and I pore over Google Earth, looking at details, noticing that Mr. Green Jeans is not in the road, so we were either gone for the year or off to town when the photos were taken. The remains of Doc's house still perch on the cliff, but the Bryants' home has already been plowed under. Unfortunately, we do this virtual traveling right before we go to bed and once I shut off my iPad and try to sleep, my heart starts its familiar thumping. It's a shock to process such a clear visual of what had only been a memory. I toss for about an hour and then give in to my faithful sleep companion, Ambien, which I haven't used for weeks.

A woman in my book club recently asked me what it was about maps that captured my imagination so. It was a good question and I fumbled the answer. I really have never thought about it. Perhaps it comes back to an issue of control. Maps help me see clearly what is, so I understand what's around me and can see—and prepare for—what comes next. They illustrate my world and help me mentally contain it.

I have always been able to lose myself in maps, such as the Geological Survey's map of our section of land, especially the version Harlan gave us when we first bought this place, showing who owned the surrounding parcels. That helped me figure out which fence marked whose property and what meadow ended in which ridge.

Russ gave me a three-dimensional relief map of Colorado several years ago and Josh gave me one of just the Spanish Peaks area; both maps hang next to one another in the cabin and I often stop and run my finger over them, tracing the bump that is our peak. When Ed and Gwyn's grandsons, Connor and Caden, visit, they like to track their journey from Fort Collins down here, feeling their way along the Front Range, then the Wet Mountains, finally to the peak.

"That's the whole world," Caden said of the map when he was about four.

"No," big brother Connor corrected. "It's just Colorado."

Caden was right, though. Maps really are the world in a package, with annotations.

Maps show the wrinkles on the face of the Earth and define human development—the roads cutting into the forest and over the rivers and around the mountains. The beauty of our place is that humans haven't built much up here— it's too far and too difficult. In fact, our land is on the U.S. Forest Service's maps of Colorado's "roadless areas," parts of the world that remain remote and welcoming to wildlife. I sometimes wish we had bought in a more populated area, with a better road. That would probably have been a good real estate decision and it would have made it possible for us to be here throughout the year.

But then I go sit on our deck and look for miles and see no signs of humans, and I hear only the birds and the gurgling of the creek and feel the warmth of the sun, and I know this place is sacred. It remains a paradise, a blessing, a daily resurrection, holy and wholly good.

24: Pockets of Gorgeous Hope

A series of brutal winters, late spring snowstorms, and high winds have snapped the tops off most of our burned trees and felled some of our remaining green ones. Our surviving forest now is full of ten-foot-high splintered trunks and dead branches.

These weather extremes are all part of a worldwide pattern, fueled by higher temperatures that lead to intense storms so unique they've earned their own names: "bomb cyclones," "rain bombs," "flash droughts," and "smoke waves."

A bomb cyclone hit Colorado in the spring of 2019—a snowstorm trapped in a whirl of dangerously high winds hundreds of miles wide. Photos from space looked like a white tornado was eating my home state. Our mountain got the tail end of it, with killing winds and heavy snow that cracked and crumbled evergreen boughs and downed entire trees. They survived the fire and floods, but this was one onslaught too many.

Rain bombs—unrelenting downpours that pound a region, saturate the soil, and cause flash floods—sneak up on us in the summer. A forecast of rain might mean nothing, or it might mean a deluge. And when that deluge lands on a landscape stripped by a forest fire, you have a disaster on top of a catastrophe. Even mild rainfalls can cause flooding the first years after a fire; rain bombs turn cow paths into rushing rivers.

Flash droughts have affected states to our north, the Dakotas and Montana, a weather phenomenon in which a precipitation-rich period is followed by a short phase of extreme dryness that quickly sucks up all the moisture, killing crops, and reducing range land for cattle. In Montana, it has led to multiple wildfires in recent years.

Smoke waves are the toxic clouds that blow over neighboring cities and countrysides in the wake of a wildfire. Environmental scientists from Yale, Harvard, Colorado State, and the University of Michigan use the term to refer to two or more consecutive days with high air pollution from wildfires. Writing in the journal *Climate Change,* they estimate that "more than 82 million individuals will be affected by Smoke Waves in the future, with Northern California, Western Oregon and the Great Plains bearing the greatest burden."

In 2018, we once again evacuated when the Spring Creek Fire came within 25 miles of our cabin, burning 108,000 acres and filling our mountain valley with noxious fumes. We were not at risk of fire, but the air itself was dangerous. We were escaping a smoke wave.

Every walk here is a reminder of what we have lost. I thought that would get easier with time, but it gets harder. It's clear parts of this land are not going to recover anytime soon, perhaps never. And our spring storms have shown that even the trees that lived through the fire are at risk from extreme rain and snow.

A third of the recently burned forests in the American West will never regenerate, according to research in the journal *Ecology Letters*. These forests were too dry to begin with and their fires burned too hot, which killed not only their trees but their seeds and, therefore, their ability to grow new trees. When forestry scientists studied burned forests in Colorado, Wyoming, Washington, Idaho, and Montana, they found no seedlings—none, zero—in these sites. These forests will most likely return as shrublands, a consequence of climate change. And we will have lost the beauty and health benefits and animal habitats of huge swaths of America's natural treescapes.

In the midst of all of this, periods of calm settle over out mountain and lull us into thinking things are as they once were, an easy sell because above all else, we want normal. We want to believe that the climate-related disasters we keep seeing are exceptions that will somehow resolve themselves. This is idiotic, but it is also human. How can we give up hope? What then?

Pockets of gorgeous remain—the meadow and its looming evergreens, the mountain when it catches the golden sunrise, the rushing stream, the silence, the milky way clearly visible in the night sky.

Early summer rains have been gentle and fruitful, leaving lushness in their wake: waist-high grass and profusions of colorful flowers and birds. The peony by our deck in recent years has had blooms at least six inches in diameter. Our iris bulbs have tripled and blossomed into fist-sized purple flowers. Our hollyhock is taller than me and has scores of silky pink buds.

A few delphiniums have sprouted on the ridge, probably brought in by a bird, 5-foot tall purple lovelies that are a natural sign of rebirth.

Weeds continue to lurk, but they're fewer and more controlled. We've planted more grass on the ridge, topping it with hay from the meadow, and that has been growing well, crowding out the thistle and mullein. Gwyn and Ed continue spraying. We pull mullein by hand and clip the blooms off thistle.

Some aspen groves are now more than 10 feet tall. Our seedlings are prospering—at least the ones we can find. The tallest are a bit more than five feet high. But the locusts and scrub oak are taking over everything they can and some of the areas where we planted baby trees remain impenetrable. It is a battle to keep up.

Ed and Gwyn are the champions of seedlings up here, with more than a thousand. Joe and I buy new plants every year but the 75 Douglas firs and ponderosa pines we planted the first year are our only successful crop. Our aspens all died, as did our junipers, the latter being perhaps a good thing because we learn, after we get them, that they burn quickly and easily because of their aromatic oil. The firs and pines we ordered this year arrived just as Joe broke his ankle and we had to put off our trip to the cabin, so Ed and Gwyn planted those as well.

At least a third of our original crop of trees are green and growing, even in often oppressive heat. We have found only a handful of dead seedlings. Ed keeps the trees all watered regularly, and we try to keep weeds from overtaking them.

We model ourselves after Wangari Maathai, winner of the 2004 Nobel Peace Prize, who began the Green Belt Movement in 1977, which is responsible for planting 30 million trees in Africa. The organization began as a way to improve the lives of women; Maathai and her colleagues discovered early on that one important way to do this was to plant trees, which provide fuel, food, shelter, and income to help sustain women and their families. In doing so, they demonstrated the essential nature of trees to our health and livelihood.

I chose a quote from Maathai's Nobel Lecture as my epigraph for this book because it explains my focus better than I can: "We are called to assist the Earth to heal her wounds, and in the process heal our own."

The trees Maathai, who died in 2011, planted will provide immediate aid to people in her native Kenya, but they also are long-term climate coolers and filters that can benefit living creatures throughout the world, including those of us in our little Colorado valley. Likewise, the trees we're planting can help mitigate warming elsewhere, although it will be a while before we get to 40 million. It's all connected. We all share one fragile planet.

The universality of our experience keeps me grounded and rattles me at the same time. I am not alone, and that's tragic. I love this land, as did the indigenous people who lived here hundreds of years before white settlers tried to tame nature, as do farmers in the Andes, or shepherds in Asia. But I have resources unknown to people in Africa, or Puerto Rico, or Central America, or even parts of the United States. I can walk away from this land and go back to a comfortable house elsewhere. I can buy new trees and I still have the resources to tend them.

When disaster struck, I lost a dream. Others have done that too, but many also have lost their homes and livelihoods.

· · ·

Last fall, we looked up at the mountain with Russ's telescope, wanting a better view of the bits of green we can see in the burn scar. We assumed weeds had colonized up there as well. Instead, we saw aspens, just starting to change color, the mountain regenerating itself.

Alleluia!

And, remarkably, we have finished several things on our cabin to-do list. We now have new wooden blinds, freshly painted walls, and oak window trim inside. Joe replaced our front deck, which had several pieces of rotted wood, and used the old boards to make a little pergola for his handmade swing.

We had to get a new refrigerator two years ago and the experience defined the challenge of our existence here. It was delivered to Walsenburg because the big transit companies will still not drive up our road. It was too big for Mr. Green Jeans, so Ed met us in town and delivered it to our front door. He and Joe dragged it up our steps and installed it, gas hook-up and all. Ed and Joe are getting a bit old to be carrying refrigerators but who else is there?

Last year, our water heater fizzled out, and Joe ordered new parts and fixed it, causing only one small fire. It's a do-it-yourself land, and the consequences aren't always pretty.

We thought improving the cabin would lift our spirits, that at least we can control this 480-square-foot interior patch. But it was always about the land here. The cabin was just our vehicle for enjoying it.

Our health is all over the place. Gwyn and I are more than four years past our cancer diagnoses, with no recurrences. Joe has had fewer episodes of cholangitis and he manages those with pain killers and antibiotics. Ed's digestion is a mess and his diet has shrunk to a few staples that usually don't bother him. My emphysema has worsened and is now severe, with a precipitous drop in lung function since the fire. I keep hiking, with pitifully frequent stops for breathing, which takes a great deal of the joy out of a walk, but my doctor is astonished I am doing what I do, so I plan to keep it up. Use it or lose it.

Wayne Cascio, writing in *Science of the Total Environment* in 2018 warns that as wildfires increase in number and severity, more and more people will face greater risks to overall health. Sadly, we may not find out the full scope of those risks until others who live through a fire are diagnosed and the scientific connections are made. That is until others, like us, are already sick.

I long to walk in the forests we once had, but they're gone. Gone.

When we first built our cabin, we visited with neighbors regularly and shared meals and lively conversation with Ed and Gwyn several times a week. Now Joe and I spend most of our time up here alone.

We see bears, but they have enough food and leave us alone. Last year we had two pairs of moms and twins, one with cubs so tiny they couldn't get their paws far enough around a tree to climb it; they tried but they kept sliding down. One afternoon, a wee cub poked her nose in our side screen door, probably lured by my chili. I yelled at it to scat and she did, her back legs next to her ears, her front legs touching her butt. Another little guy nosed around Mr. Green Jeans, either chasing a mouse or smelling the peanut butter Joe uses on mousetraps he puts in the engine to keep the critters from chewing our wires. We clicked our car alarm and he ran, then came back. We hit the alarm again and he ran, then came back. After the third time, he stayed away—or we didn't see him return.

While these are not threatening encounters, my heartbeat still goes into overdrive with each one, choking off my breathing, and sending me into a coughing spasm. Rationally I don't feel I am panicking, but the physical symptoms are clear.

As I write this, my chest constricts, my hands begin to shake.

I replace earplugs with my iPhone ear buds and listen to an app with the sounds of rain to calm me into sleep. You'd think a woman who has weathered as many floods as I have might avoid the sound of falling water. But what I hear on my app in normal, how rain is supposed to act, and therefore tranquil. I usually sleep through until morning light. But if I wake in the night, I awake to fear. I am reluctant to take off the silent security of my ear buds long enough to go to the bathroom. My bladder has the last word and luckily all is quiet inside and out while I am up.

If I don't hear a bear, I feel safe. Fear is what threatens me most now.

My anxiety has been formalized, given a name by The American Psychological Association: climate anxiety disorder, also called eco-anxiety, climate change distress, climate grief, and ecological grief. Whatever the name, it is real, it is increasing, and it is a serious threat to our emotional wellbeing. The terms typically apply to people who have been affected by a natural disaster linked to climate change—hurricanes, tropical storms, earthquakes, and wildfires. The symptoms: depression, fear, anxiety, PTSD. But even those whose experience only includes learning about and believing climate-change risks, even if they're not directly involved, tend to be more depressed and stressed than those less informed.

Those who spend the most time in nature and show concern for plants and animals are the most likely to be worried about the climate crisis, perhaps because they have seen its effects most closely, according to research by Sabrina Helm and colleagues at the University of Arizona Institute of the Environment. In fact, climate scientists are among the most affected by climate anxiety. Helm says: "Climate change is a persistent global stressor."

In 2017 alone, wildfires burned more than 9 million acres of America's forests, and scientists are unequivocal about the connection between this unprecedented level of burning and the climate crisis. "Human-caused climate change caused over half of the documented increases in fuel aridity [the degree to which a climate lacks the moisture it needs] since the 1970s and doubled the cumulative forest fire area since 1984," wrote John Abatzoglou of the University of Idaho and Park Williams of Columbia University in the *Proceedings of the National Academy of Sciences (PNAS)* in 2016. Note that word: *caused.* He is not saying this is just a connection. Climate change *caused* by humans has doubled the area that has burned since 1984. Humans > climate change > forest fires.

Every year is hotter than the previous one, with all the hottest years recorded since 1880 occurring since 2005. "Scientists have known for some time that climate is a key driver of forest fires; records from the past and present provide strong evidence that warmer temperatures are associated with spikes in fire activity. Therefore, recent increases in wildfire activity as the planet warms are not a surprise," wrote Brian Harvey, of the School of Environmental and Forest Sciences at the University of Washington, also in *PNAS* in 2016.

The Southwest, Rocky Mountain region, northern Great Plains, Southeast, and Pacific Coast are the most at risk of future fires caused by continued warming trends, according to researchers at the Center for Forest Disturbance Science of the U.S. Forest Service in Athens, Georgia.

And these fires are making us sick. A heat wave in Moscow in 2010 and subsequent wildfires led to more than 2,000 deaths. Mostly these were from cardiovascular, respiratory, urinary, genital, and nervous system diseases among people over 65, according to 2014 research published in the journal *Epidemiology*. Pollution from fires is projected to cause an additional 339,000 deaths a year worldwide, based on research by the Menzies Research Institute at the University of Tasmania, published in 2012 in *Environmental Health Perspectives*.

Each fire makes the news for a while, then disappears when it is contained and, supposedly, the story is over. Mass communications scholars call this the Issue-Attention Cycle, a phenomenon in which a story saturates the airways and the consciousness of the public and then is just as quickly replaced with a new and fresh story, as though the first one had never happened. Those of us in the middle of fires, though, know that it's all just beginning. When the cameras and reporters leave, we're left with the aftermath.

This is not normal. In the 25 years from 1950 to 1985, the United States had only nine historically significant wildfires—those that have destroyed more than 100,000 acres. By contrast, *nearly 6 million acres a year* have burned in the ten years from 2008 to 2018, according to the National Interagency Fire Center. That's a burn nearly the size of New Jersey—every year.

The scientists who studied the air above Yosemite's Rim Fire in 2013 suggested one solution: increasing controlled, or prescribed, burns that are intentionally set and carefully monitored by forestry professionals to clear dead wood and to create open spaces between trees. The difference between these and today's wildfires is significant: Controlled burns create five tons of biofuel (burning underbrush and trees) per acre. By comparison, a wildfire burns 30, or six times as much, creating six times the pollution and destruction.

Planned burning was once a staple of land management for the continent's earliest settlers, Native Americans, and their forests were often well groomed as a result. When Europeans first came to this country, they were impressed by the quality of the woodlands in the East, not realizing that they were the result of centuries of carefully planned burns.

Controlled burns make the land more usable, improve wildlife habitats, and reduce the effects of naturally occurring fires. If a wildfire hits an area that has previously been burned, it will move more slowly and be less hot and thus will be easier to contain. The U.S. Forest Service advocates using controlled burns, and has done so historically, but it doesn't have the budget to follow through on the scale that is needed.

Our risks have increased and our protections against it have decreased.

Meanwhile, people like us are trying to rebuild and renew the priceless treasure that is our land. It's a slow slog made even harder by watching our experience repeat itself all over the globe.

The damage to this forest affects the climate of the entire planet. And the climate of the planet affects this forest.

We've seen climate change happen from our little deck. We've watched trees across the meadow die from drought and from beetle damage, from fire, and from the shock after the fire. We've seen their burned hulls falls over from weakness and we've seen healthy trees uprooted by wicked winds. We've watched weeds and shrubs take their place.

We've seen our gentle creek dry up in the summer heat and then swell into a destructive torrent after an extreme storm, killing the willows in its path and turning the meadow into a swamp.

We've seen eagles build nests in towering trees and we've seen the trees and the nests incinerated. We've watched hungry bears looking for acorns after the drought has killed the crop. We've watched as the numbers of elk, songbirds, even our dependable hummingbirds, have dwindled year after year.

We've seen people, once gregarious and communal, turn into themselves with depression, illness, and overwork.

We've seen our hiking trails turn into a chaotic mash of downed trees, weeds, and prickly locust bushes. We've watched as our world has shrunk, as the woods we once roamed have disappeared, as the glades that looked like they were landscaped by the gods have become logging roads to carry out dead trees.

We have seen all this. We are witnesses to a changing climate, to what it is doing to our mountain, and what it is doing to our planet.

But we've seen the firs and spruce and pines that survived along our valley thrive and welcome at least a few eagles and hawks back to the neighborhood. We've watched our meadow grow into a lush buffet of grasses and wildflowers. What songbirds we have are colorful—red, blue, yellow, orange—and songful, and we've seen them gorge themselves on choke cherry bushes bursting with fruit. We've watched a progression of mama bears wander the Bear Highway with their cubs, a different family every year. We leave them alone and they do the same with us.

Birth, death, chaos, resurrection, hope, despair. It's all there, right outside our remote little mountain cabin.

Someday our seedlings may become soaring wonders like the trees they replaced, queens of a healthy forest, but that depends on how the planet warms and changes, and how we tend it.

I can envision many different futures, and I increasingly despair of believing the most hopeful one. In that one, the one I pray for, the one I once took for granted, my grandsons look up at a batch of giant trees in a Colorado valley and tell their grandchildren:

"Your great-great grandparents planted those."

Notes

Epigraph
Wangari Maathai, Nobel Lecture, December 10, 2004. Used with permission from the Nobel Foundation, January 6, 2020.
nobelprize.org/prizes/peace/2004/maathai/26050-wangari-maathai-nobel-lecture-2004/

Prologue
The Spanish Peaks region of southern Colorado is nearly 2,000 square miles full of the remnants of ancient volcanic activity—mountains, hills, and buttes built of igneous, or molten rock. The dikes are the most notable and obvious, but the region also has volcanic cones, plugs, and lava sheets atop high mesas.

For photos and more details about this unique region, go to *Spanishpeakscountry.com* and search "The Great Dikes."

For a geologist's perspective on this unique region, check out Ross B. Johnson's 1968 paper, *Geology of the Igneous Rocks of the Spanish Peaks Region Colorado*, available online at *pubs.er.usgs.gov/publication/pp594G*

Chapter 1
The Natural Resources Defense Council offers a PDF on "The West's Changed Climate" at *nrdc.org/sites/default/files/west.pdf/* The Council's "Climate Facts" page presents results of more than 50 scientific studies linking forest fires and climate change at *nrdc.org/sites/default/files/fwest.pdf*

The National Centers for Environmental Information provides current and historical data on droughts throughout the United States, searchable by month and year. For the interactive drought map, go to *ncdc.noaa.gov/sotc/drought/201306*.

John T. Abatzaglou and Lauren Parker tracked increases in temperature in the West from 1895 to 2016. Their paper, "Climate Change and the American West," was published in April 2018 in the *Idaho Law Review*.

Chapter 2
Multiple studies, primarily in Japan, have demonstrated that *Shinrin-yoku*, or "forest bathing," can positively affect all five senses, plus improve our immune responses. An overview was published in 2010 in *Environmental Health and*

Preventive Medicine, available through the National Institutes of *ncbi.nlm.nih.gov/pmc/articles/PMC2793347/*
You can see why we get mesmerized by the mountain when you watch the video of its dance with the clouds at *patriciaprijatel.com/2018/01/20/the-mountains-dance-of-the-clouds/*

Inside Ecology magazine explains the science of soundscapes in relation to biodiversity—the healthier the land, the more diverse the ambient noise: a variety of birds, streams, even wind. And the more diverse the ambient noise, the healthier the people living nearby. Details at insideecology.com//09/28/do-you-hear-what-i-hear-the-science-of-soundscapes/

Chapter 3
Prijatel also means *lover* in Russian. But we are not Russian, so we're just friends.

I have a video of our cabin at *patriciaprijatel.com/2018/01/31/our-little-mountain-cabin/*

Chapters 4-7
More than 22,000 lighting fires are reported in the United States each year, mostly in the Northwest and Rocky Mountain Regions. Dry lightning, or lightning not accompanied by rain, caused the East Peak Fire. Data from the National Oceanic and Atmospheric Association show that fires caused by lightning burn more acres on average than those caused by humans. *lightningsafety.noaa.gov/fire.shtml*

Check out *Wildfire Today* for a map of the East Peak Fire, showing areas of intensity, at *wildfiretoday.com/2013/06/22/colorado-east-peak-fire/*

NASA's Earth Observatory shows a view of the fire from space at *earthobservatory.nasa.gov/NaturalHazards/view.php?id=81479*
The National Interagency Fire Center in Boise, Idaho keeps statistics on wildfires in the United States. The largest, in Alaska in 2004, burned 1.3 million acres. At least one historically significant fire has burned each year since then. Every year since 2010, the U.S. has had two or more fires that have burned more than 100,000 acres.
nifc.gov/fireInfo/fireInfo_stats_histSigFires.html

The U.S. Forest Service and its Wildland Fire Assessment Service offer an online tool to predict and monitor wildfires at *www.wfas.net*

National Forests describes the role of aspens in fire fighting at *fs.fed.us/wildflowers/beauty/aspen/grow.shtml*

Since 1984, the number of forest fires has increased by 1,000 percent, according to Park Williams, of the Center for Climate and Life at Columbia University. Climate change causes increased temperatures, which cause droughts that cause forest fires. See an interview with Williams about the California wildfires of 2017 on PBS at *pbs.org/newshour/show/climate-change-is-part-of-californias-perfect-recipe-for-intense-wildfire*

For a video of what we saw as we escaped, and the devastation we returned to, go to *patriciaprijatel.com/2017/12/11/june-19-2013/*

Chapter 8
Huerfano County birders have seen bald and golden eagles, the sharp-skinned hawk, the Cooper's Hawk, the Northern Goshawk, the broad-winged hawk, Swainson's hawk, red tailed hawk, gulls, owls, pelicans, songbirds, hummingbirds, and scores of others. The Colorado County Birding site offers a county-by-county list of current sightings at *coloradocountybirding.org/ByCounty.aspx?CountyID=29*

While aluminum melts at 1,220.58 degrees Fahrenheit, it boils at 4,566 degrees. More aluminum facts at *livescience.com/28865-aluminum.html*

Photos of the pirate's burned face, compared to his healthy green countenance the year before the fire, are at *patriciaprijatel.com/2018/01/01/the-pirate-on-the-mountain/*

Chapter 9
The Colorado State Forest Service monitors wildfires throughout the state and works with landowners and communities to mitigate fire and flood damage. Their services include sand bags, seedlings, and technical advice. More information is at http://csfs.colostate.edu/wildfire-mitigation/

Before and after shots of the fire are at *patriciaprijatel.com/2018/01/01/the-east-spanish-peak-before-and-after-the-fire/* and at *patriciaprijatel.com/2017/12/11/before-and-after/*

Chapter 10
Thistle and mullein are both on Colorado's list of noxious weeds. The state has multiple types of thistle—bull, musk, Canada, plumeless, and Scotch—but only one type of mullein—common mullein. The full list is at *colorado.gov/pacific/agconservation/noxious-weed-species*

Chapter 11
The idea of going into the woods to die is ascribed by many as part of Native-American tradition. I could find nothing to back this up. The United States has

573 federally recognized Indian Nations, in 36 states, according to the National Congress of American Indians (*ncai.org*). These nations have distinct cultural practices, but all revere their elders so would likely not send them off to the woods, although some recalcitrant old folks might do it on their own. I suspect this myth came from an old Western movie.

Chapter 12
The Black Forest Fire of 2013 destroyed 488 homes and caused $420.5 million in insured damage, according to the Rocky Mountain Insurance Information Association as reported in the *Denver Post* on June 14, 2015. A year earlier, the Waldo Canyon Fire destroyed 347 homes and caused $460.3 in insured claims. Both were in the Colorado Springs area. I can find no record of insurance claims for the East Peak Fire, which burned "only" 10 homes and four outbuildings, but devastated 13,572 acres of forest.
denverpost.com/2013/07/09/black-forest-fire-caused-85-million-in-damage-to-homes-assessor-says/

Chapter 13
Recently burned soils can retain nutrients that might otherwise be lost, including nitrogen, phosphorus, and sulfur, according to the Forest Encyclopedia Network. While being destructive to trees, wildfires can rejuvenate grasses and native species of wildflowers and shrubs.
nau.edu/~gaud/bio300w/frsl.htm

Chapter 14
The National Park Service notes that, while a black bear's sense of smell is extraordinary, it is actually difficult to measure precisely; nevertheless, the NPS says that, conservatively, a black bear is able to smell at least two miles away. This is about seven times greater than a bloodhound and comes, in part, from their large noses, the inside of which (the nasal mucosa) is 100 times bigger than ours. More details are at *nps.gov/yose/blogs/bear-series-part-one-a-bears-sense-of-smell.htm*

Shots of our ratty old bear and its footprints on our deck are at *patriciaprijatel.com/2017/12/12/our-neighbor-the-bear/*

Chapter 15
The Centers for Disease Control counted 108 deaths caused by cattle between 2003 and 2008 and provides case reports such as: "In August 2007, a man in Iowa aged 45 years who was working alone in a pasture was attacked by a bull that had been bottle-fed and raised by the family but, according to family members, had become more aggressive recently. Nobody witnessed the incident, but the man was able to call his wife for assistance on his cell phone before he died and told her he had been attacked. According to the state

medical examiner's autopsy report, he died of blunt force injuries to the chest. Online at *cdc.gov/mmwr/preview/mmwrhtml/mm5829a2.htm*

The *National Geographic* article, "Canada Mauling Reflects Spike in Human-Bear Encounters," byReed Karaim, is accessible online at *news.nationalgeographic.com/news/2014/05/140508-bear-attack-mauling-grizzly-black-wildlife-animals/*

For an account of the Rim Fire research on toxic air, read "Wildfires May Be More Toxic Than Scientists Thought," in *The Atlantic*, June 23, 2017. *theatlantic.com/science/archive/2017/06/wildfires-release-more-pollutants-than-scientists-thought/531333/*

Chapter 16
A cubic foot of granite weighs 175 pounds. The rocks we saw were 2-3 times that size.

Chapter 17
An adult black bear is 50 to 80 inches long, from nose to tail, and weighs as much as 800 pounds, with males being larger than females. Average weight of females is 150 pounds and of males is 250 pounds. Cubs usually stay with their mothers for 16 months. Only 5 percent die of natural causes—the rest die from gunshot, road-kills, and other interactions with humans. Cubs and yearlings can die from starvation.

More bear facts from the University of Minnesota's Bear With Us page (*bearwithus.org*) and the New Mexico's Wildlife Education worksheet (*wildlife.state.nm.us*).

For more about bears in Colorado, including the history of grizzlies in the state, check our Laura Pritchett's *Great Colorado Bear Stories* (Riverbend Publishing, 2013).

Chapter 18
Colorado's most common flies are black flies, deer flies, and horseflies, all of which can—and do—bite humans. They are most prevalent in warm, moist conditions. The heat in the cabin may be what lures them in the late fall. According to the Colorado State Extension (*extension.colostate.edu/topic-areas/insects/*), controlling them is difficult. And horse flies apparently only bite at higher altitudes, such as ours, but they can be "nasty biters." We have the welts to support that.

Chapter 19

Breast cancer density patterns are often grouped geographically, with women in specific areas tending to have denser breasts than those in other areas. Researchers at the University of Florida now say this could be because of air pollution, which they link to dense breasts. And breast density is an established risk for breast cancer. The university's press release on the subject is at *news.phhp.ufl.edu/2017/06/02/in-the-air/*

Seven to eight people out of 100 will develop post-traumatic stress disorder in their lives, according to the National Institute of Mental Health. It's not clear why some develop PSTD and other don't but living through a dangerous event and continued stress are key factors. Exposure therapy for PTSD gradually reintroduces the patient to the trauma to control their fears. I accidentally did this, with mixed success. Years after the fire, flood, and bear, I am still easily spooked by noises in the night. Our bear interaction and our worst flood happened in the dark, making me especially anxious after the sun goes down. nimh.nih.gov/health/topics/post-traumatic-stress-disorder-ptsd/index.shtml

Chapter 20

Common mullein has a "list C" designation under the Colorado Noxious Weed Act, meaning it must be eradicated, contained, or suppressed. Because each plant can create up to 250,000 seeds and it has a deep taproot, it is difficult to contain. The Colorado Department of Agriculture recommends a combination of cultivating the area where the plant grows and replacing it with grass, introducing seed-eating weevils, hand pulling, and using chemicals. Each musk thistle head produced up to 1,200 seeds that can last in the soil up to ten years, and most plants have a dozen or more heads. The CDA recommends pulling or mowing the plant before it flowers, using herbicides, or treating with the musk thistle rosette weevil. We've tried it all but the weevils. *colorado.gov/pacific/agconservation/common-mullein*

For the photo I took of the hawk against the burned mountain, go to my blog at *patriciaprijatel.com/2018/01/31/a-hawks-view-of-the-east-spanish-peak/*

Chapter 21

Eagles typically have one to three fledglings; clutches of four are possible, but rare. They use the same nest year after year. Building a new one takes one to three months and is built by both males and females. The National Eagle Center in Minnesota (*nationaleaglecenter.org*) tracks both bald and golden eagles and has extensive data on our national symbol and her cousins.

Chapter 22

Storms have not increased in their frequency but have become more intense as a result of global warming, says the Union of Concerned Scientists *(ucsusa.org/global-warming/science-and-impacts/impacts/hurricanes-and-climate-change)*. That means that extreme events like hurricanes Harvey, Irma, and Maria, in such close proximity, will continue and probably increase.

According to NASA an increase in Earth's temperatures will result in more droughts as well as more intense storms, including an increase in wind speeds. *(earthobservatory.nasa.gov/Features/RisingCost/rising_cost5.php)*,

Chapter 23
Forests are the "largest forms of carbon storage in the world" and "deforestation accounts for up to 15 percent of global emissions of heat-trapping gases," according to American Forests. Without the forests we are losing to fires, the Earth will get even hotter and our air will be less filtered. Details at *americanforests.org/explore-forests/forest-facts/*

The National Centers for Environmental Information keeps statistics on the number of fires in the country, searchable by year at *ncdc.noaa.gov/sotc/fire/201713*

Chapter 24
North America has lost 3 billion birds in a little less than 50 years, according to research in the journal *Science*, due to factors such as the disruption of ecosystems and loss of habitat. The study is online at *sciencemag.org/content/early/2019/09/25/science.aaw1313*

CITATIONS

Beyond Storms and Droughts: The Psychological Impacts of Climate Change, Clayton, Susan; et al. Washington D.C. (2014): The American Psychological Association and EcoAmerica.

"Climate Change Impacts on Wildfires in a Mediterranean Environment," Turco, Marco; et al. *Climactic Change*, 2014.

"Critical Review of Health Impacts of Wildfire Smoke Exposure," Reid, Colleen E.; et al. *Environmental Health Perspectives*, 2016.

"Differentiating Environmental Concern in the Context of Psychological Adaption to Climate Change," Sabrina V.Helm, Amanda Pollitt, Melissa,A.Barnett, Melissa A.Curran, Zelieann R.Craig. *Global Environmental Change*, 2018.

"Estimated Global Mortality Attributable to Smoke from Landscape Fires," Johnston F.H.; et al. *Environmental Health Perspectives*, 2012.

"Evidence for declining forest resilience to wildfires under climate change," Stevens-Rumann, C. S., Kemp, K. B., Higuera, P. E., Harvey, B. J., Rother, M. T., Donato, D. C., Morgan, P. and Veblen, T. T. *Ecology Letters*, 2018.

"Future U.S. Wildfire Potential Trends Projected Using a Dynamically Downscaled Climate Change Scenario," Liu, Yongqiang; Goodrich, Scott; Stanturf, John. *Forest Ecology and Management*, 2013.

"Human-Caused Climate Change Is Now a Key Driver of Forest Fire Activity in the Western United States," Harvey, Brian, *Proceedings of the National Academy of Sciences*, 2016.

"Mortality Related to Air Pollution with the Moscow Heat Wave and Wildfire of 2010," Shaposhnikov, Dmitry; et al. *Epidemiology*, 2014.

"Particulate Air Pollution from Wildfires in the Western U.S. Under Climate Change," Liu, Jia Coco; et al. *Climatic Change*, 2016.
"Wildland Fire Smoke and Human Health," Cascio, Wayne E. *Science of the Total Environment*, 2018.

Climate Grief Resources
Climate Psychology Alliance *climatepsychologyalliance.org*

Climate Psychiatry Alliance *climatepsychiatry.org*

Eco-Anxious Stories *ecoanxious.ca*

Good Grief Network *goodgriefnetwork.org*

International Community for Ecopsychology *www.ecopsychology.org*

Psychology and Global Climate Change: Addressing a Multi-faceted Phenomenon and Set of Challenges. Report of the American Psychological Association Task Force on the Interface Between Psychology and Global Climate Change (2011).
apa.org/science/about/publications/climate-change

Yale Climate Connections *yaleclimateconnections.org*

Acknowledgements

Special thanks to the village that helped me create this book and, most important, supported me along the way. Sharelle Moranville used her significant skills as a writer of fiction to guide me in my storytelling. Ann Hinga Klein provided writing insight and environmental savvy. Polly Flug read this with the eyes of a seasoned journalist and editor. Jennifer Bedell jumped in when InDesign and I were not understanding one another at all. Phyllis Jennings and Gail Stilwill offered encouragement when this was just a bit of a babble. Matt Strelecki reviewed my cover and told me it was better than I thought. Jeff Bruner, the Fussy Librarian, shared the wisdom of the bookseller. My Facebook friends helped me choose a title and cover illustration and expressed eagerness to read the book. (Please, please!) And the Binders always had an encouraging response as I muddled my way through this process.

To all those who lived parts of this story with me—my family, friends, neighbors, and the blessed firefighters—I hope I have done justice to your memories of the fire and to your connection with the land we share.

About the Author

Patricia Prijatel is the author of *Surviving Triple-Negative Breast Cancer* and *The Magazine from Cover to Cover*. She is the founder and editor of the *Positives About Negative* blog; her All Is Well Blog is published on *psychologytoday.com*. She lives mostly in Iowa and sometimes in Colorado.

www.ingramcontent.com/pod-product-compliance
Lightning Source LLC
Chambersburg PA
CBHW060038030426

42334CB00019B/2382